Always an
Orphan

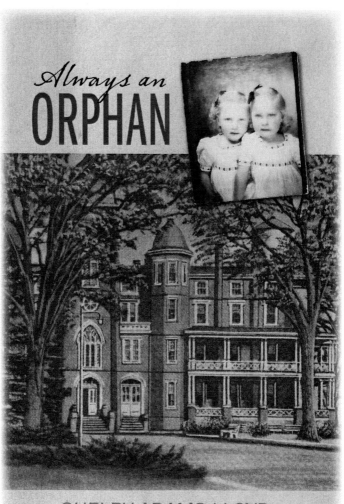

Always an
ORPHAN

SHELBY ADAMS LLOYD

Bink Books

Bedazzled Ink Publishing Company • Fairfield, California

978-1-945805-15-8 paperback

Cover Design
by

DESIGNS

3 1703 00639 6701

Bink Books
a division of
Bedazzled Ink Publishing Company
Fairfield, California
http://www.bedazzledink.com

Dedication

My grandchildren love hearing stories about my orphanage home and I dedicate this book to them first. They are amazed at how I grew up. They can pass on these stories of their Gram and Aunt Jo Ann to their children and grandchildren. My special grandchildren are Jennifer, Brad, Jaclyn, Madalyn Jean, Jordan, and last is Haydan. I cannot forget my great grandson, Bryson, who is an important part in my life. I love them to the moon and back because they always love me as much as I love them. These seven young grandchildren are important people in my life.

I have to include my own children because they are my precious babies I brought into this world with Donald and they have our genes and they passed them on to my wonderful grandchildren. Our children are Lynn, Donald (Don), and Rhonda. These young people I love with all my heart and today they are still my babies.

The most important person in my life for fifty-eight years is my wonderful husband and best friend, Donald. You have put up with me for all these years and I hope we can be together for another twenty years at least. I sort of doubt it but hey, why not try. Love you with all my heart and thanks for putting up with me while I sit at the computer writing four fiction manuscripts and one biography/memoirs about my life growing up at Oxford Orphanage, in Oxford, North Carolina.

My sister, Jo Ann Adams, was with me during our time in the orphanage and she went through the same turmoil as me. We still have that fear of rejection when we think of our family. I definitely have to dedicate this book to her. "I love you Jo with all my heart and yes, to the moon and back." We will always be orphans, however we don't care who calls us that.

Then there are those who didn't give up on me and kept telling me to write about my life in an orphanage. Kathy

Holbrook, you were the first one to tell me to write this book and the one who kept telling me, "Do it, do it, just do it, Boo-boo." This is what she calls me at times and I love hearing it from her. She didn't give up on me and I have to add her to the list of people I dedicate this book to. "You are the first friend I met in Southport and I love you to the moon and back, also."

Linda Lange, you wanted to read what I had written and you've been so gracious to read and edit this manuscript several times. You became a good friend to me even before you and Steve joined Trinity United Methodist Church. Then I asked you to help in the church kitchen every Wednesday when Becky and I did the cooking for members coming to dinner on this special night of the week. Of course, you accepted and we still do it together.

We became good friends and your life was not far from mine. The only difference I see is that you were not in an orphanage. Our past has been a drawing card for both of us and we can sit and talk about it. Thank you for being my friend and helping me with this manuscript. You know everything about me now and you still love me. I think you are a wonderful, loving friend and I'm here if you ever need me.

Becky Felton, you have been my friend since we moved to Southport. There could be no better friend than you. You are there for me when I need a good laugh or cry. You will drop whatever you are doing to help me. I love you to the moon and back over and over again. You told me that your grandmother lived in my home many moons ago, in the early years when the orphanage first began. This makes me so proud to know that part of your family is part of my family of orphans. I love you Becky Felton, no one could have a better friend than you.

I have never gotten mad at you and I hope you can say the same except when I do something stupid. Even when Donald and I move back to Raleigh, you are not that far away. There is the phone or e-mail we can use to stay in touch. You will always be a dear friend of mine whether we are together or not.

Good friends never go away, only distance that causes us not to see one another often.

I have to dedicate this to my dear friend who has gone on to be with our Lord, Bert Felton, Becky's husband. "I will miss you and when we start cooking again on September 16, 2015 for our Wonderful Wednesday night dinners at our church. I will miss you walking in the back door with a large smile on your face, reaching for your apron.

Bert, I will see you again when I enter the gates of glory. Save me a place so we can sit and talk about our Wonderful Wednesdays and the people who came for a meal at Trinity United Methodist Church of Southport, North Carolina.

I have pictures to put in the book when an agent grabs up this manuscript. I am hoping there is a publisher out there who will publish the book. These pictures are old, but they belong in this book.

Linda Lange, thank you so much for helping me get this manuscript ready to send out. You have spent many hours on it and I am indebted to you for helping me get it finished. You are my adopted sister. Thank you, thank you, and thank you for your long hours. You truly are a great adopted sister to me.

Oxford Orphanage Alma Mater

Written by Myrtle Peacock, music teacher,
at the orphanage while I was there.

Hail to Oxford, dear old Oxford
Noble Fair and strong
With her colors red and back,
We praise her with a song.
First thou art in worth and beauty;
First where e'er we roam
Sing we then our Alma Mater,
Oxford Orphanage Home.

CHORUS
Children of the great republic
One in voice and heart and will,
Strong and noble in the future
Swell the chorus, let it thrill.

Praise this shrine for ev'ry Mason
Let no voice be still.
The have made our Orphanage Home
With a royal will.
In Our colors, bold and stirring,
Red and black unscarred;
Oxford Orphanage, Alma Mater,
Always in regard.

CHORUS
Children of the great republic
One in voice and heart and will,
Strong and noble in the future
Swell the chorus, let it thrill.

Prologue

WHERE DO I begin telling the world how I went through childhood without too many flaws? Many of my friends have asked me to put my life on paper so others can see how orphans were treated in my home, Oxford Orphanage, in Oxford, North Carolina. It is now called The Masonic Home for Children.

I always think my life is boring, and to my knowledge, I haven't done anything outstanding in my life. I've been a wife, mother, and of course I have always been an orphan since the age of three. For those who don't know anyone growing up in an orphanage, it is different from growing up in a normal home. Of course, I love my home the same as everyone loves their home. My home housed three hundred plus children when I was growing up.

There is no way any of us could be bored because there was always something we had to do at work, school, and play. We didn't even know the word *bored* meant because there was someone to be with at all times. Each of the orphans who grew up with me have gone on and excelled in their schooling and professional lives. We were determined to excel after leaving our home and we pushed ourselves to go to college and then have a profession.

Why am I opening up my life to the public? How will I feel if this book is published? Will I be ashamed of pouring out my life to everyone? I'm doing this because growing up as an orphan in Oxford Orphanage is a life different from most people I know.

Do I want the world to know me because I'm not ashamed of living in an orphanage? There are others in worse condition than I have ever been in, but they probably didn't live in an orphanage.

Who wants to read about an average woman who is seventy-nine writing about her life as an orphan? I am sitting here in tears, thinking about my genetic family. I don't know if I have the courage to tell what my heart has held secretive for many years. Do I start by telling the reason I was placed in my orphanage home? It is easy for others to say I can do it, however they did not grow up in an orphanage.

If I lie, it's not my life's story. There are a few things I don't want others to know about me so I'm afraid to put those experiences into words for the entire world to know. I know for sure that I was a good kid growing up in the orphanage and I never did anything to be ashamed of. Well, maybe when I ran away, but I don't care if people know that part of my life because that part is certainly not boring.

Yet my heart is full of fear at this very moment. Fear of not being entirely honest with my story. Each orphan had different episodes throughout their childhood. The boys have an entirely different story to tell because they were not as sheltered as the girls were.

So, here I sit contemplating my childhood. The fear of opening up my heart I've felt for years is about to come forward. I don't know how hard it's going to be writing about my life as an orphan. My subconscious will suddenly come to the front of my brain and I will have to start writing about growing up in the orphanage.

Please enjoy my story. I have spent time trying to recollect everything that happened to me and my orphan family. It is a place for young orphans like me back then to grow and become good and decent adults. Orphans are a part of my every being, orphans that I love with all of my heart. There are some orphans who hated our home, but then there are orphans, who, like me call the orphanage their home. They have a story of their own to tell.

This story is one of love I learned from my many orphan brothers and sisters that became a part of my life back then and today. If I didn't have their love in my heart I would feel wretched and I couldn't live without it. I love these people in a strong way and no one can ever take that from me. I will die knowing I have a loving family of hundreds of brothers and sisters and hopefully we will be together when we enter the gates of Heaven.

I was an orphan at the early age of three, I am an orphan today, and I will be an orphan tomorrow. However, I know one thing for sure, I have more than enough orphan brothers and sisters and there is no way I can ever be completely isolated from them. All I have to do is pick up the phone and call, write, or go see one of my family members of orphans and I won't be lonely again. There is no rejection from my many orphan brothers and sisters, only LOVE flowing to the moon and back.

One

I NEVER THOUGHT about being an orphan, but I have been one since I was three years old. Of course, my sister and I didn't understand what an orphan was when we were little. As I recall, no one ever used the word *orphan* to either of us. An orphan I was back then, an orphan I am today, and an orphan I will be tomorrow until death takes me home to my Lord.

Our Mama died at the age of twenty-six on September 5, 1939. She left two small girls with no mother and a dad who was a drunk most of the time. Since that day my sister, Jo Ann Adams, and I, Shelby Jean Adams Lloyd, have been more or less on our own. Two and three years of age left alone with a dad who drank alcohol like it was water.

Let me tell you about my mother that we love even though we didn't know her. Grandma named our mama Cleo Jane Fish. When she married our dad her last name became Adams. To my knowledge I don't remember anything about her before she died, since I was just three years old. There are flashes, but I don't know if someone told to me about my mother or not.

When Mama died we had no idea what was happening. I do remember someone holding me up to her casket so I could see her. She was lying in a bed of white satin clouds. The pillow her head rested on was also satin and I remember it being white, fluffy, and glistening looking.

Her bed looked like clouds, so soft and pretty, especially when the sun is out. Mama had on a mauve colored velveteen dress with a shiny pin near her breast. I remember it sparkled and I could see the hues of reds, greens, blue, and purple when the sun shone on it. It was beautiful and when I close my eyes I can see that pin today.

Mama's beautiful blue eyes were closed. Her hair had little waves all over her head where someone had set it. It was the newest craze in the late thirties. Her beautiful red hair was curly, unquestionably curly, and almost unmanageable, just like mine. It wanted to go its own way, and the finger waves helped to soften her face. This was the fashion then and I've been told that Mama loved to have the latest fashions.

I can see her when I close my eyes. My unmarried aunt had a picture of her on the mantel, in the living room, at Grandma's house. A beautiful lady inside and out so I've been told. She was a young woman who should have lived many more years. I've been told she wanted to be busy all the time. I am the same, even today at the age of seventy nine. If I happen to be seated, I want something to do like crocheting or reading. Even sewing is better than nothing.

I wanted that smile of hers to tell me everything was going to be okay. Not understanding at the age of three, I probably thought she was sleeping. If someone would shake her hard enough she would pop open those big beautiful blue eyes and give me one of her loving smiles. I wish I could remember Mama's face because all my life I have wanted to remember her. It still nags at me because I cannot remember her.

I know I saw her in her casket because I recall the shade of pink her dress was and the broach she had at the crease of her breast reflecting different colors. I remember all of this and no one told me. In fact, my married aunt was shocked when I told her what I recalled. I just wanted Mama to see me and smile with those big blue eyes.

Someone told me that I kept touching her beautiful red hair. Red hair is a trait from Grandma's side of the family. So many of the Stephenson girls had red hair. I've been told by many people that I am the carbon copy of Mama. Not just in looks, but my makeup is a carbon copy of her. However, my hair was blonde, not red as I was growing up. Of course it is now dark blonde and gray.

After Mama died our dad went into the army. I was told by his sister that he beat Mama the day she died. She had asthma and I guess the beating brought on an occurrence of not being able to breathe and it caused her death. He was a sorry-ass man who loved his booze more than his family.

I would give anything to have had Mama during my time growing up. We were too young to be without her. We needed her to teach us manners and show us how to cook and clean. We needed her to love us and give us a big hug. Jo and I would love to remember how she would hug and kiss us.

I had a dream about Mama not too many years ago. In the dream she was in her casket and Grandma kept telling me to go see what she wanted. Grandma was conveying to me not to be afraid because Mama had something to tell me. Even Papa kept pushing me toward that casket. In the dream everyone was dead but me.

I was petrified to walk over to her. I wanted to stay with Grandma and not have to go toward that casket. I was afraid of going forward and couldn't understand why she wanted to tell me something. I was so scared to the point of wanting to run out of the room.

In the dream she was smiling at me. Believe it or not, I remember that smile and I believe God gave me the chance to see Mama. If she looks the way I saw in that dream, she was a beautiful young lady. Her eyes were a radiant blue, blue as the sky on a sunny day. There was a smile in them and Mama's face glowed with love coming from it.

THE DAY MAMA died Jo Ann and I went to our aunt and uncle's house. They lived at the top of a long hilly road that led down to Papa's house. My aunt told me how she was holding my sister in her arms and I held her other hand as we walked down that long road to Grandma's house shortly after Mama was buried. It wasn't an extremely long road, however a three year old little girl whose legs were short took forever to even see Grandma's house. It was hard . . . so . . . hard to keep up with my aunt. I'm sure she was tired of holding Jo Ann in her arms, too.

I guess my uncle had the car for some reason. Of course, they may not have had a car in the year nineteen-thirty-nine. Back then most people didn't have one. There were not many cars on the road in the early forties, especially the country roads that were not paved. Most farmers used their money for machinery to help with the farming, not cars.

Before we got to Grandma's house my married aunt told me I was asking her to hold me. My short legs were tired . . . so . . . tired . . . walking down that lengthy . . . dirt . . . road. It was hard to keep up and I'm sure I thought we would never get there. She couldn't hold both of us. She said I was crying, wanting Mama to come back. Evidently, I cried for days and no one could please me. She said I kept asking for Mama and it was a desperate time for my sister and me. We had no idea where our parents had gone. We were two small children with no parents to love us again.

Two

JO ANN AND I ended up living with Grandma and Papa. I guess we were too much for my aunt because she had two children of her own and they needed her attention. My uncle was a farmer and if he didn't have a good year, things were hard to come by, even buying food for the table. I'm sure our aunt canned a lot during the summer because they grew all the vegetables they ate.

Papa was an aristocratic farmer and didn't want to be responsible for raising two little girls who were left without a mother at the age of two and three. Grandma gathered us in her arms and loved us the way Mama had done. Grandma was there to see us grow until she passed away when Jo Ann was seven and I was eight.

In Grandma's house lived my unmarried aunt and uncle. I didn't call them aunt or uncle, I called them by their given names. My unmarried aunt was probably nine and my unmarried uncle was probably around seven when we went to live with Grandma.

We were happy for a few years. I don't recall being unhappy and most of those years are not present to me today. I know we were happy enough because Grandma was an angel according to people of Willow Springs, North Carolina. She would give us a big hug when we got up each morning and then a big hug and kiss during the day. I wish she had lived to see us get married and have our own children.

I remember watching Grandma wash our clothes in a big black pot in the back yard before we had a washing machine. Using a scrubbing board, she bent over that big, black pot scrubbing all the clothes that were soiled. Then she hung them on a line, one that Papa made for her. There were two lines strung from the house to fig tree as I recall. I can close my eyes and see her hanging the clothes with clothespins as I write about her. Both lines would be filled by the end of the morning. She would try to stand straight enough to reach the line. She was so hunched over from arthritis and it was hard for her, but as I recall she never complained. She was a beautiful lady and I still love her so much.

The sheets always smelled so fresh when she changed our bed each week. I love getting between them and going to sleep while smelling the sweet smell of sunshine. Even today I would love to hang my sheets and towels on a line outside to get that smell of freshness the sun gives, but no one does this anymore. We are too busy doing other things and of course, neighbors would complain about it.

Grandma worked hard making a home for her family. She was our angel from heaven and she lives in my heart today. I can see her beautiful face when I reminisce about those days. I can visualize the way she walked due to rheumatoid arthritis that ate away at her muscles daily. She wore her hair in a knot at the back of her head and it was black, sprinkled with gray. She had beautiful eyes that sparkled when she hugged me. Her arthritis was bad, but she did everything in the house and outside. During the winter months I would go with her to the sweet potato mound to dig up some of those delicious potatoes for dinner. She would get on the ground and start digging through the dirt and up popped a sweet potato.

One of my uncles was in the Navy during the Second World War and he would send chewing gum home for the family. Sugar was hard to come by in those days because of the war. Jo and I loved that gum and Grandma would give us a piece once in a while from the trunk she kept it in. The smell of it before it entered our mouths had a sweet and wonderful smell to it. Oh, the taste of that Dentyne gum, slightly burning with the cinnamon flavor, was a special treat for us. I would chew that gum all day and when Grandma told me to spit it out I would cry. Of course, it didn't have the same taste after hours of chewing it, but I wanted to keep it because it would be a long time before we would get another stick.

She never gave up on anyone who couldn't fend for themselves. She was our special Grandma Angel. A great woman who didn't mind being in pain daily. She was so drawn over, causing her to live every day in pain from that horrible disease.

I never knew how much pain she suffered until my daughter, Lynn, was diagnosed with rheumatoid arthritis. I know now how much suffering there is with this disease. It causes the joints to be painful each time Lynn moves. Then there are time when a flair-up appears and it sends her to bed. She gets so sick and no matter how good she wants to feel, she can't because of this terrible . . . sickness she undergoes daily . . . with . . . pain.

There are times when she has to stop taking her medication because it is causing something else to go wrong and the medication has to be changed again and again. Lynn suffers all the time, but you never hear her complain. She keeps it to herself just like Grandma did, but I can tell when she's in pain. Her eyes don't sparkle like stars when this happens to her. She suffers daily just like her great grandma and there is nothing that frees her completely of the pain.

WE DIDN'T HAVE a bathtub or toilet for some time when we were young. Papa added on to the house and had them installed in the new bathroom some time before we went to the orphanage and it was a large bathroom. Of course, we had to walk through Grandma's bedroom to get to it but we didn't care, at least we didn't have to go outside to the toilet. At night we used a slop jar if we had to get up. That way we wouldn't wake Papa and Grandma.

Before we had a bathtub Grandma gave us a bath in a big tub on the back, screened-in, porch on Saturday nights because we were going to Sunday school and church on Sunday morning. We also had a bath in that same tub on Wednesday night. We didn't have another bath unless we were extremely dirty for some reason. Then we get an extra bath during the week.

I'm sure it was hard for her due to that awful disease, but she was a beautiful young grandma that Jo and I loved. She was a wonderful Christian lady and her cheerfulness was catching. No one can ever take her place in our hearts. Even today I am proud of my loving grandma and someday I hope to be with her in Heaven.

Jo and I probably were like her own children because my aunt and uncle were only a few years older than we were. This angel worked hard raising her two children and two grandchildren. RA didn't make things better and being drawn over, due to that horrendous sickness, had to be hard for her. In fact, they didn't have the medicine in those days to help people with this terrible disease.

One day Jo and I spent the night with another girl from school. I think that maybe she was kin to us in some way. I don't even recall her name. Regardless, we came home and Grandma found bed bugs in our dirty clothing. She had to take all of our clothes and boil them on the stove. Then she took the sheets off the bed and boiled them in the black pot out in the back yard. She didn't scold us because we didn't know this friend had bed bugs in her house. If she had let it go we would have bed bugs at our house. Grandma was a clean freak, the same as Mama. Jo and I are now clean freaks, too. That trait was passed down to us and we have passed it down to our children.

Three

WE LOST GRANDMA when I was eight years old and Jo Ann was seven. She died November sixth, 1944. I was a snotty-nose kid who loved playing outside rather than sitting in the house. I was settled in the third grade, but I don't remember my teacher's name, however I enjoyed reading and writing. This was the year I found words captivating, triggering me to love reading.

In the country where Papa and Grandma lived was nice because you could sit on the porch at night and watch the stars twinkling from above. Even the small light from the fireflies penetrated the darkness. It was so peaceful sitting in the swing and see the night become dark during the summer. You could hear the frogs crocking, wanting it to rain. It was such a peaceful time in our lives.

There were no cars flying up the road and the quietness of the evening was like paradise. How pretty those stars were as I sat there dreaming as a child. We would catch those fireflies in jars and hurry and put the lid on it so we could see those fireflies give off light.

I always wanted to see a star fall from the sky. I finally saw one when I was thirteen and I was exuberant, it thrilled me so much. We were home for vacation that summer and Jo and I were sitting on the front porch talking, looking at the stars, and dreaming about growing up and getting married. How calm I felt when I was there, hoping Papa would finally show us the love we had for him. But he never showered us with his love and we were disenchanted because of it.

THERE WERE PEOPLE everywhere in the house the night Grandma died . . . like ants . . . Some were in the kitchen, some in the living room, and some were in the bedroom. I didn't understand why they were there. Most of the guests were in the bedroom where Grandma lay extremely sick. Jo Ann and I were at a loss, seeing so many visitors in our home at one time.

There was no laughter anywhere in the house on that cold November night. The stillness in the house was like a death . . . ready . . . waiting . . . to take shape. I didn't know a death was taking place as I stood looking out at the lonesome world beyond the window.

I remember Grandma's kitchen on that cold November night, looking out at the dark sky with only stars glowing brightly overhead. The stars were giving off a small amount of light. Being in the country, people didn't use outside lights, except on the front or back porches. When it became dark, they went inside. There were no street lights in the country and in 1944 most of the country roads happened to be unpaved. You were lucky to live on a paved road.

We were hanging out in the kitchen with my cousins, who were as mystified as we were. I only knew Grandma had been extremely sick for over a week. She stayed in the bed the entire time. When we returned from school each day she called us to her bedroom to ask how school had gone that day. Then she would tell us to do our homework before we went to bed. She kept us on our toes about doing well in school.

Dinner time arrived with tables full of good food and everyone was helping themselves. Let me tell you, when I say food on the tables, I mean a lot of food that came from nearby wives of farmers. Talk about desserts, I remember seeing my favorite, coconut cake. There were several of them and I knew there would be some for me tomorrow when I got home from school.

People had brought ham, beef roast with potatoes soaking in gravy, fried chicken, and chicken in different sauces such as barbecue. There were lots of veggies that came from jars that were kept in the pantry. These veggies were grown by these kind people, then pickled and canned by women who, not only worked in the fields, but also picked these veggies to can. Canning takes time doing this process. Nowadays I freeze my veggies and only can tomatoes different ways. I still make plum and pineapple jam for my grandchildren plus Donald and me.

Jo Ann and I were standing at the window, looking out at the dark sky. It wasn't late, probably six-seven o'clock, but it was a black, dark world outside, and we couldn't see past the window. It was as though God let the darkness fall on Papa's house.

Most of the people in the house on that cold November night were people we knew or family members. That was the reason we didn't understand why they wanted to be in Grandma's bedroom. No one had said anything about Grandma dying. It was a mystery to all the children wandering around the kitchen. The noise was null and void, no talking, no laughing at all. The quietness was overwhelming to us.

As I reminisce, there were maybe twenty or more people walking around the different rooms of that large, old farmhouse. Some were in the living room, talking quietly, not to disturb Grandma. The eyes of visitors were showing a sign of sorrow and death. There was not even a smile on the faces of our family members.

People were sitting in chairs, talking softly to one another and watching as Grandma tried to breathe. Papa was sitting next to the bed holding her hand. No one had told us that she was that sick. We didn't know she was going away like Mama.

I was so troubled that night. I remember clearly how people were acting, not talking to us, and only patting us on the head. I had a terrible ache in my heart, knowing something bad was about to take place. Of course, I didn't realize it was Grandma. She had been sick for over a week and I thought she would soon be smiling at us when we left on the bus for school. She would always give us a love pat us on our behind before we got on that bus each day.

The guests were waiting . . . waiting . . . for Grandma . . . die . . . I don't remember seeing Papa's face or if he was crying. Being a child, I probably didn't think to look at him. My married aunt came to the kitchen and told us to go and see Grandma. We went to the bedroom where she lay and it wouldn't be long before she would be gone.

I remember I could hardly see her face. She was covered with the quilt around her face. Grandma was a beautiful lady even with the humped back. Her smile was a beautiful one that I remember today. She was my grandma and going away like my Mother had done.

A nurse came into the bedroom and walked around the family members to get to the bed. Then she took a mirror and held it under Grandma's nose and mouth and said, "She's gone." This happened when we heard Grandma grasped. Then she walked away from the bed.

I looked around at my cousins and said, "Where is she going?" I didn't understand since she was sick. Obviously, I already knew what was happening, but I didn't want to accept it. It startled me, causing me to start crying. My heart was breaking because I had a feeling of something bad taking place when we were in the kitchen. I didn't want to think of Grandma leaving Jo and me.

Jo Ann and I had been with Grandma and Papa since our mother had passed away. I wanted her to stay with us so we would have someone to love us. I loved this woman who worked hard every day, even on Sunday, because there was always cooking to do for the family. I don't remember her sitting down often except to eat her meals. Oh how I wish she had lived until I grew up and got married. I can see her with her great grandchildren, holding them in her lap and giving them a big bear hug like she did to Jo Ann and me when she was alive.

She loved us enough to take us in when our mother died. I'm sure she was tired by the end of each day. Grandma was a special lady and we loved her so much. She would tell us she loved us to the moon and back and I thought it was so silly back then, but I use those same words today when I tell my children and grandchildren how much I love them.

I'm sure she loved Jo and me to the moon and back because she would give us that bear hug us and plant a kiss on our dirty cheeks. This lady who loved us and said the word *"Love."* It's a beautiful word and it comes from the heart in the form of happiness, joy, and affection. Love is important and it would be hard not to love someone as special as Grandma.

A FEW DAYS after Grandma died, some men brought her back home in a casket. The casket had satin sheets just like my mother's casket. They rolled that casket to the living room where people could walk by to look at her. I didn't quite understand, but I'm sure I knew she was dead.

I do remember I was afraid to go to the living room. I didn't know if she would suddenly sit up and grab me. One of my cousins was several years older than me and he told me she would grab me and I would be dead like her. This caused me to stay far away from the living room. To get to my bedroom I would walk on the wraparound porch to the sitting room and open the door.

She had those same finger waves in her hair that Mama had. I didn't understand death because I had never been told anything about it. At night someone would sit with Grandma and people called it a Wake. I didn't understand what they meant by it being a wake because she had her eyes closed. Why would someone sit with her if she was just lying there . . . dead? I had never seen anyone dead except Mama that I can recollect at that young age. I was too young and didn't understand when I was told Mama had died. I didn't want to understand or believe that Grandma was dead, too.

Grandma was there for two days and there was always someone sitting with her. One day they lowered the top of the casket and rolled her out to the yard. They then opened the casket for people to take pictures of Grandma. In fact, I have a picture of her in the casket. Now that Grandma was gone would there be anyone to love Jo and me. We were so frightened, there wasn't anyone to love us the way Grandma had every day.

After the pictures were taken, they closed the top of the casket and put her in a large car and left. It wasn't long before we were in a car going somewhere. We pulled up at my church and I was beginning to think it must be Sunday. I had on my pretty pink dress, patent leather shoes, and white socks with lace around the tops. I was dressed for church and I only wore these clothes on Sunday.

We went inside the church and all of my family members were there. We sat on the front rows and heard the preacher talk about how good Grandma had been to people. We sang songs, some I enjoyed singing and when I turned around I saw people crying. Why were they crying? Were they unhappy knowing Grandma was gone, too?

Finally, some men came to the front of the church and closed the casket again. They took the flowers that were over that brown casket and laid them on the floor. Then they rolled Grandma to the outside door. Some men picked up the casket and took her to the cemetery where a large hole had been dug. They lowered the casket in the ground and covered her up.

I was scared seeing the men put Grandma in such a large hole. What if they put me in a hole like that? How was she going to breathe with the casket closed? Wouldn't the dirt cause her to be cold since it was November? How could I breathe if they put all that dirt over me?

I was almost hyperventilating, watching the men shovel dirt on Grandma's pretty casket. It was scaring me to the point of losing my breath. I tried to take in air but I couldn't. I had reached the point of almost passing out due to not breathing. My married aunt saw me and rubbed my back gentle. I came back from being petrified and breathing became easy once again. I started crying because I wouldn't see her again. My heart was aching because of the love I had for her. I was unhappy because she had left Jo and me the same way Mama had.

How could we live without someone loving us? It was devastating for Jo Ann and me. Even though we were too young to understand everything that was happening at a fast pace, it was hard on us. We were unhappy because within five years we lost the two women who loved us. We were alone again and this time we had no idea where we would end up because Papa didn't love us the way he did our cousins.

AFTER GRANDMA DIED things were unsettling for the family. I remember Papa being away a lot on the tobacco market since it was winter. We were a burden to him and he chose his sixteen-year-old daughter to be our guardian. She wasn't equipped to handle two children at such a young age. She tried hard but we didn't pay attention to her. She was too young to be a mother responsible for two small girls. We didn't recognize what was happening to us at that time. She was only a teenager and still in school, so was our uncle. He was only fourteen years old.

I've been told we didn't cooperate with her when she was scolding us. Accordingly, she had a hard time making us behave. We were just kids and loved playing tricks on her. I remember how we would laugh at her and run outside where she couldn't catch us. That mean streak would hover over us and we enjoyed every moment of it. We snickered when she couldn't find us.

We hid from her outside and wouldn't come when she called. We waited until she went inside the house before we showed our faces to her with a big smile. Then she would smile back at us because she knew we were teasing her.

She did the cooking, washing, ironing, and cleaning. She had a hard time getting us to do our homework. I vaguely remember some of this, I probably was told after getting older. At that time we were upset because Grandma was gone, never to give us a kiss on our dirty cheeks or a bear hug again.

A week or two went by and we were still with Papa. As you know a week is a long time for a child. He was a farmer and kept the workers in the fields planting tobacco, cotton, and other crops. There was a lot to do on the farm and he had to oversee those doing the work. He had plenty of men helping him, probably my uncle and some black men and women. Even some teenagers helped with the work and Papa paid them an hourly wage, but not during the winter.

During those years Mexicans weren't coming to the United States legally or illegally. I don't know when they started crossing the border into the United States. During those years the black people and family members helped to grow the crops. Most of them lived on the farm or close by.

Papa traveled up and down the southern part of North and South Carolina, leaving my unmarried aunt to be a mom to three people. She finally quit school and so did my unmarried uncle. They both worked on the farm and my unmarried aunt cooked the meals and kept our clothes clean. She did all the housework plus working in the fields along with others. She put in a lot of hours doing everything she had to do with no help from anyone. No one hugged her or gave her a kiss on the cheek. No one told her they loved her as I recall.

I have to admit she was busy, never having the time to mourn the death of her mother which had only been a week or two. I know she cried a lot during this time and it caused Jo and me to be unhappy for her. Frankly, she had no time for herself. She was like a maid for her daddy. I never thought too much about her doing all she did in any given day. Now that I look back on those years, she was our angel on earth after Grandma was gone.

Thinking back, it was a huge burden for her, she had just lost her mother. I do recall that Grandma died on her birthday which was November 6, 1944. I recall seeing my unmarried aunt crying when we were told that Grandma was gone. Her sobbing was heard throughout that large, overcrowded farmhouse. It was hard for her to comprehend all that was taking place. She was only a sixteen-year-old kid herself.

Four

ONE DAY PAPA took Jo and me to his sister-in-law's home. He had all our clothes packed in suitcases and was planning to leave us with her. My memory tells me it was the last week of November. We had been uprooted once and we didn't want to leave our unmarried aunt. She had become a mother to us. We loved her and knew she loved us because she treated us with love. She would even stop working and play with us at times.

Our hearts were broken once again because we didn't really know this great aunt of ours. She had come to the house on occasions but we didn't pay attention to her. She was there to see Grandma and Papa, not two snotty nose kids that were dirty from playing outside. We always played outside, riding our bikes or walking. Sometimes we would go to the pond to see if fish were jumping out of the water. During the wintertime, we couldn't see them because it was too cold. Yet, when spring arrived, they would be jumping like crazy. Papa would fish and bring several to the house for us to have for a good seafood meal.

Sometimes we went to see our uncle who had a store down from Papa's house. He would always give us a piece of candy when we went to visit him and his daughter. His daughter was our age but they didn't live there long before he moved his family.

Since we were not obeying our unmarried aunt Papa thought it best for us to leave our home and not return. This woman's husband died before I was born, I think he had the lung infection, tuberculosis. She had one son and he was older, already in high school, probably in our aunt's class. I hated living with her because she had both of us doing housework and dishes every night.

She was harsh on us when we cried due to the sadness we felt in our heart. She was unwilling to care, scolding us for crying for our beloved grandma. We were not accustomed to her house and living with her and her son caused us to be lonely except when we were at school.

At that time, we were too young to understand everything. We had been uprooted twice since I was three years old. Papa didn't tell us the reason we were being sent to his sister-in-law's house. Our hearts were hurting so bad we cried when we pulled into her driveway. We didn't understand the reason for Papa taking us away from our home.

I don't know if anyone tried to talk to us at this time. I was old enough to understand and so was Jo Ann. We were so sad, tears forming daily because we were sent away from the only home we remembered. We missed our aunt and uncle and we missed our bed. We thought we had done something outrageous for Papa to treat us this way.

Why would be the question we would face for many years? We were never told the reason he left us with his sister-in-law and we never asked, knowing in our hearts he didn't want us. This rejection was probably the first time we knew what was happening.

WE WENT THROUGH the motion of living with this woman daily. She didn't give us a hug or kiss that I remember. Jo was so timid at that time and she found it hard to express herself to this woman. I wasn't timid at all . . . but I . . . would . . . not talk to . . . her. She wasn't my aunt, only a distant kin by marriage. The next several months there were a lot of tears falling from our eyes. Tears would form most of the time when we were alone at night in those twin beds we slept in. There was no one we could talk to. No one cared if we were sad and no one came to see us. No one cared if we were being treated good or not.

I wasn't able to tell Jo Ann how much I was hurting because I know for sure she felt the same way. We were two lonely children thrown out of the house for some reason. In fact, even today I don't understand why Papa gave us away.

When we realized how we were treated, it was too late to correct. We were a rejection and evidently, there was something wrong with us from the time Mama and Grandma died. I didn't know what it was because we looked like other people.

From this point on we had a feeling of rejection, but we didn't know why we were so unhappy. It would come to us later in life after we were grown. We went through our entire childhood being unhappy because Papa didn't love . . . or . . . care . . . for . . . us. At that time, we were two children alone, not knowing what we could do or where we could go. If only someone had told us that God was looking after us each and every day of our entire . . . childhood.

I REMEMBER THAT horrible Christmas when we were staying with this great aunt. We went caroling on Christmas Eve which I enjoyed. Of course, Santa was coming later, after we had gone to bed and I was excited.

We dressed warmly and walked the road to homes nearby to sing carols. Hats were a must with ear muffs and gloves. Back then the weather was colder than what it is today. At least it seemed colder, then again, maybe it was because I was a child.

Even though it was extremely cold, we enjoyed walking to homes and singing about the birth of our Christ Child and the angels watching over Him. Neighbors would walk outside to hear us sing carols to them. It made them happy to see their neighbors fighting the cold weather to come by and serenade them.

You have to remember homes in the country were not next door where you could run over in a matter of seconds. Also, the roads were dark with no lights except for houses, which were way down the road. I don't remember if we used flashlights or not. To be sure, some of the people had flashlights because of the darkness. The road our great aunt lived on happened to be a paved one which helped a lot when walking that dark night.

Coming home, we got ready for bed, excited because Santa would soon be here to give toys to Jo and me. The lights were out in our room, and we heard a noise at the window. It scared both of us to the point of almost fainting from fear. We looked again and saw Santa Claus at the window with a flashlight to his face and that scared us even more.

That moment in time never left me and as I grew older, I hated what Papa's nephew had done to us that dreadful night. He was only a teenager, but it's etched in my mind even today. It was wrong of him to scare two small children that way. I can still see him at the window with the Santa suit on.

We were with Papa's sister-in-law for maybe three-four months. During the Christmas season we were still sad because Grandma was gone and we were living with someone who didn't love us. It was a painful time for Jo Ann and me because we received no love whatsoever. I'm sure Papa's sister-in-law felt some sort of kindness toward us, but as small children we never saw it.

Maybe you think I don't remember any of this, but you're wrong. I remember very well what went on in that house. I can still recall the rooms and where they were located throughout. The dining room was large and I had to dust it every week. She had a very long and large table with chairs that had to be dusted. Then there was a china cabinet that was huge and it was hard for me to dust. Then there was the tea cart that had to be dusted. It's funny because no one ever used that room. No one came for dinner during the time we were there.

Jo dusted the living room and we both dusted our room. Her son did his own room. I don't know who ran the vacuum cleaner or if she had one for hardwood floors back then. I think she either swept or mopped the dust from the hardwood floors. I shouldn't complain about her cleanliness since I am a clean freak myself and so is Jo Ann.

When Christmas came I don't remember anything I received from Santa, maybe the riding pants we got. They were the fashion that year for young children. I remember getting a bag of fruit and candy. I don't remember if we got anything else. I don't think we got anything from Papa that year.

I don't remember Papa coming to see us during the time we stayed with this great aunt. My family was not one to show affection to others and there were no telephones to send messages. If we were sick, I don't remember what happened. Maybe we were healthy little girls and didn't have to go to the doctor.

So, we stayed those months without even seeing Papa or a member of our family. We had been dropped off and no one cared whether we were happy, scared, or sad. Since we had been used to having Grandma around all the time we were miserable every day we stay with this great aunt.

Five

WE WENT BACK to Papa's the end of March or the first of April. We were glad to be home and not staying with this great aunt anymore. The great aunt was really okay because when I was older I realized she was teaching us what needed to be done in the home place.

However, we thought she was mean when we were small children. She used to drop by when we were home on vacation to see us. She was always friendly and wanted to know how we were doing at our orphanage home. I could see that she did love us, but evidently it was hard for her to show affection.

Accordingly, I was home where I belonged, at least for a little while. Since we were home, we assumed we were going to stay. I was eight and Jo was seven years old. We shared a bedroom at home and we cuddled close when the winters were so cold. We were thirteen months apart in age and people used to think we were twins. We were always together during those few years before we were sent to our orphanage home.

One afternoon shortly after we came home from school a lady was there to visit Papa. She asked if we would like to live with lots of other children. I had no idea what she was talking about, but other children sounded good to me. Jo Ann wasn't so sure, she wanted to stay with Papa. She was still shy and didn't take to strangers well. The woman's name was Eunice Broadwell, a case worker for the orphanage. I learned this after going to the orphanage to live.

Sometime during the next few weeks Papa took Jo Ann and me on a road trip. It was only a day trip, but it was a long one. We traveled through Raleigh and then we were on a road that was hilly and winding. I thought we would never get to where we were going.

Papa slowed down when we came to the town of Oxford, North Carolina. We were on a road where there were large, beautiful homes. I was enjoying seeing them, dreaming maybe I would live in a house like them one day when I grew up.

Donald and I go that way to the orphanage each year for homecoming and I always look at those beautiful homes. Most of them have been renovated inside and out.

We turned on a road that led up to a large building. We orphans call it *the main road.* It was so beautiful and I loved it as soon as I saw it. Big oak trees swayed gently in the breeze and there were some teenagers walking around.

There was grass everywhere around and under those trees. I had never seen so much grass. Living in the country most of my early years, I saw more dirt than grass because the fields were turned over during the winter months to be prepared for planting in the spring.

I wanted to sit under those trees and dream my special dream of Mama and Grandma coming home to Jo and me. It was still hard to accept the fact we would never see them again. I didn't know where we would end up next.

Papa got out and went inside the large building for some reason. He came out and started the car again. We went only a short distance and pulled up at another large building. Papa got out and went up the steps to the inside. Jo Ann and I stayed outside until Papa came to get us.

A woman was standing near the sofa as we walked in. Papa introduced us to Mrs. Tomblin and she was wearing a nurse's uniform. She had the prettiest white hair I had ever seen. Of course I hadn't seen many women with white hair. Even so, she was a beautiful, older lady who had become stout due to age and eating more than necessary. But she stood straight and was very becoming. I liked this beautiful woman from the beginning. She called for someone to come to the front and a young teenager appeared and told us to follow her.

The hallway didn't have carpet, instead it was a rubber mat that ran all the way from the living room down a long hallway. You could hear your shoes squeak as they took each step on that rubber mat. The hall was dark, no windows which made us have an eerie feeling. Then we saw a room with a funny looking chair in it. It was so high and would be hard to climb on it. At least there were windows in the room. There were cabinets against the wall of the room.

Finally we walked into a large room and the teenager called it a playroom. The room also had windows, making it not so depressing. Some of the toys were broken but some were okay. The checkerboard was on the bottom and there was a small box with chips in it. Jo got down on the floor and started playing checkers all by herself. Some of the chips were lost so no one had enough of the black and red chips to play an entire game.

The teenager left us alone and went somewhere else. We looked around and saw another container with toys and there were books on the coffee table. I picked up a book to look at and Jo got up from the floor and sat beside me and looked on as I tried to read. I had learned a lot of words in the first and second grade and so far I was doing rather well in the third grade. She also knew a lot of the words since she was in the second grade.

It seemed to take a long time for Papa to talk to the nurse so I decided to walk up that long hallway to see why it was taking so long. I was ready to leave and I'm sure Jo Ann was, too. I was getting hungry and wanted to go home so we could eat supper.

I walked up that long, dark, terrifying hallway and saw the nurse. She was older than Papa, and with her beautiful white hair, she could have been over one hundred years old in a child's eyes. She looked up at me when I entered the space where she was sitting on the sofa reading a book. I looked at the title of the book and it was *Wuthering Heights*. It was a book I would probably read when I was older.

I looked at her and asked, "Where's Papa? My sister and I are ready to go home."

She looked at me, and I thought I saw tears in her eyes. "Shelby, your Papa has gone home. You and Jo Ann are going to stay here in the orphanage."

I looked at her dumbfounded. I had no idea what she was talking about.

"What's an orphanage?" I asked. The word was long and I couldn't get all of it out of my mouth to sound right.

"An orphanage is a place where children live who have no parents. That is the reason you and your sister are here." I must have been okay with what she was telling me because I didn't say anything for a long moment.

Then I looked at her, pondering what she meant by no parents. "But, I do have parents, my daddy and Papa. Papa is my Papa." I stood there looking at this beautiful, older woman for quite some time. "Why are we going to stay here with you?"

"You will stay here with me for now. Then you will go to a house where there are a lot of girls living." She smiled at me, and I turned and ran back down that long, dark hallway, hearing my shoes squeak as they touched the rubber mat. I ran to the playroom where my sister stood . . . waiting . . . for me at the door.

Jo Ann was crying by now and when I saw her I started crying. She didn't understand what was happening and I didn't either. No matter what I said, we both cried more. Jo kept saying she didn't want to stay. I didn't want to either, but Papa had gone and we didn't think we would ever see him again.

I, being a year older, understood a lot of things, but I was having a hard time digesting Papa leaving us alone with a stranger. Did someone make him give us away? Was Daddy responsible for Papa giving us to the lady with the white hair? We had no idea what tomorrow would bring. Two small children struggling for five years and not knowing where we would end up next.

This was not the first rejection I felt, but it was certainly the worse one. It hurt throughout my small body even though I didn't understand where the hurt was coming from. I was so sad, I didn't know what to do. My sister and I were in no-man's-land. It was such a deep hurt from the bottom of my feet to the top of my head. Heartbroken mercilessly because

Papa didn't love us. We didn't understand why he did this to us again. We were simply too young to understand the adult world.

Fear of rejection still plagues me. It's such a deep jolt that I will take to my grave. I don't want to have that feeling again. It's damaging to my heart each time that fear is allowed to come forward. We were so distraught, questioning what would come next.

Now that I am much older, when I get this feeling I look to God. He loves me, regardless of how I look or how I act. Knowing that He loves me is all I need. There is no fear of rejection from our Heavenly Father. He's always there for me in the good and bad times of my life, leading me down the right path. I learned a long time ago to trust in the Lord and know He loves me and all His children.

Six

FEAR OF REJECTION was implanted in me at the tender age of three even though I had no idea what it meant. It has haunted me throughout my life. I don't feel the hurt as much anymore. However, sometimes it hangs onto me like glue. I try to tear it away so I can see past the unhappiness my family left me with.

Jo looked at me and asked, "Why is Papa not coming back?" Then she started crying.

"Jo, he left us to stay here where children live and we will go to school here, too. Please . . . don't cry . . . anymore. You are going to make me cry again."

She looked at me with her unhappy small face and said, "He left us over an hour ago to get back home before dark. He doesn't want us, he gave us to that old woman."

When she said that, it hit me hard, like a slap in the face. Yes, he left us again because he didn't want us. We were left alone in a place we didn't know. Troubled by our destiny we were to swallow it up and go on from there. He was throwing us away because we had done something awful.

When a child is rejected or there is no love shown, they don't think about God loving them. That doesn't enter their thoughts, they worry about people loving or not loving them. It's so hard on a youngster to understand things the way grown-ups do.

We were alone, this . . . time . . . really . . . alone. Uprooted— again . . . left with the woman with the white hair. What had we done to make Papa hate us? When our mom died, we were alone even though our dad was there for a little while. I couldn't believe Papa would leave us with this woman.

I went back up that long, dark hallway with the rubber mat to Mrs. Tomblin and asked, "Why did he forget my sister and me? Does he not love us anymore?"

"You and your sister are here to stay. He won't be back except to visit with you from time to time. Now, go on back down to the playroom where your sister is playing."

I looked at the woman with the white dress and hair. Tears gathered in my eyes because I didn't want to stay here. Where were the children the lady had told me about? I turned around and walked back down that desolate . . . long . . . hallway to the playroom and saw Jo Ann crying.

"Don't cry Jo, we have to stay. Papa left when we walked down here a long time ago. He's gone and the woman in the white dress said we are going to live here."

Jo looked at me strangely as if I had lost my mind? "No, no, Shelby, Papa didn't leave us here forever. He has probably gone somewhere and will be back."

I knew better because the woman said so. It seemed to take forever before someone came and took us to the kitchen for dinner. We didn't do much talking, just ate our food and sat there. After everyone was finished, a teenager took us to the bathroom to wash our face, wash our hands, brush our teeth, and get ready for bed.

After bathing we were told which of the beds we were to sleep on. It was so quiet, no one stirring about. I turned and looked around. I saw the large bedroom and there were around fourteen to sixteen beds. All the beds were made of white iron like my unmarried uncle had at home, but his bed was brown. His bed wasn't as high as these, you had to get on these by putting your feet between the rails at the bottom. They only held one person and not enough room for Jo and me to share. We looked at one another, wishing we could go home. I remember looking at the sadness in my sister's eyes and there was not one thing I could do to make things right for her or me.

Five minutes is a long time for a child. It was now dark and the moon wasn't giving off any light. I could hear the wind howling, probably generating a storm outside. I knew how afraid Jo was of lightning and thundering. I felt empty, traumatized from my feet to my head. It was a spooky feeling I was having because a storm would soon come.

We had been eliminated by Papa. That night became lonely . . . so lonely . . . and . . . the fear of rejection . . . sat in. There was an uneasy feeling in both of us. A fear in me was taking shape and I was petrified. I could not comprehend it and somehow it made me feel unwanted. I still remember that fear today as I write about going to my orphanage home. It was the most disturbing terror I've ever felt.

Where was Grandma and Mama? I needed someone to hold me and give me a kiss or a great big hug. Could I live without the love of another person? Would I end up a total castoff because no one wanted me? My heart was heavy as I stood at the window, looking out at the dark sky. What in the world were we going to do? It was so hard to understand at the age of eight.

We were scared that night and sleep didn't want to come. With the storm brewing outside, lightning and thundering would soon arrive. I believe it was the worse night I have ever survived. Jo heard the storm off in the distance and it scared her. She covered her head so she couldn't see the lightning when it arrived.

Being abandoned as an adult is challenging to say the least, but a small child . . . abandonment is something . . . hard . . . to define. Empty and lost are the words I think of when I was lonely that horrifying night in April of 1945. This was almost as bad as losing our grandma. We were alone, a dark . . . dark . . .place. There was a creepy feeling in me, one that I couldn't grasp. The storm was being played out for a long, enduring time frame.

We didn't know another person in this foreign city Papa called Oxford, North Carolina. The building was so large you could get lost and never find your way out. Where were all the children the lady told us about? Was she lying to get Papa to give us away? I wanted to see other boys and girls. I was looking forward to seeing lots of children to play with. Not only did I feel rejected, the woman lied to us; there were no children here at all.

I LOOKED OUT the window at the head of my bed. Off in the distance I could see the lightning light up the sky far away. I've never been afraid of storms, but tonight I was lonely, scared to death as to what was taking shape. I was horrified and didn't understand what was happening to me.

I wanted Grandma and Mama to come back. I didn't recognize the reasoning of Papa giving us to the woman. I was brokenhearted, my heart was bleeding, and wanting someone to tell me they loved Jo Ann and me. I wish I had known Christ better during this time in my life because of my wounded heart. I was a dejected child and no one to turn to for advice. My sister and I had been pushed out of our home and no one cared for us.

Seven

A NEW PLACE, new town, new people, and nowhere to go. We were in a place the woman called an orphanage. No love to share with two little girls, age of seven and eight. I remember that first night in the infirmary and how scared and abandoned I felt. But it would be up to us to make the best of the situation. No one in this place knew how traumatized we were. They didn't care because they didn't love us. However, they didn't know us, either. We were rejected by our family of genes and not one of them cared.

Now the rejection gets stronger and longer during each year I live. Rejections for some reason comes to the front of my brain, causing me to feel the hurt all over again. It is a hurt of its own; dwelling in you, never a retreat of any kind. It's always nearby, ready to swoop upon you if you aren't careful and if your brain's not sharp as a tack. It's nearby, ready for you to be abandoned one more time.

We were odd-balls. Our family excluded us because something had been left out when we entered this world. I thought, at the time, people didn't want to show us any love because we were strange, weird looking. We were like an animal in the forest, on our own. We would have to fight for food and a place to live at a very early age.

No one would ever love us as much as Grandma. We had to admit it, move on, and grow up without our family. We could never look back or the rejection would swallow us. It was time to forget about our family, time to leave the past behind. The rejection penetrated my brain each time I thought about our family. The rejection was beginning to set in like concrete. That hurt nagging at me again . . . again . . . every day for the rest of my life.

JO ANN AND I lay in those beds for a long time, hearing the strengthening of the storm. There was a disturbing stillness all around us. The calm penetrated our small bodies to the point of us wanting to scream.

When we were at home I could hear Papa talking when we went to bed. Most of the time he was talking to our unmarried aunt who looked after us each day. They would talk, laugh, and seem to be having a great time together. It gave me a feeling of warmth.

I heard Jo crying softly and I didn't know if I should go to her or not. I could hold her and let her cry it out, but then again, I was afraid, too. After all, I was still a child myself. The bedroom became a dark, pitch blackness, but lights in the hallway were on. I could see shadows moving around. Even the shadows were creepy. There was no way to tell if they belonged to a person or animal or maybe a ghost. It was a strange mixture of people and animals I saw as I looked at the lighted hallway. It was frightening for me and I didn't like seeing them. Still, I couldn't tear my eyes away from that door leading to the hallway. I finally believed it had to be people, but why were they walking up and down the hall? Were they afraid of the storm, as well?

At home, we always kept the light on until my unmarried aunt came to bed. But now, it was pitched black all around us except for the hall. I could see the murkiness through the windows. I could hear the wind gusting noisily through the trees. A spring shower was arriving off in the distance. I could still hear the developing of thunder and lightning, getting closer . . . closer . . .

It wasn't long before the lightning was at the window, emphasizing everything in the room. Jo was afraid of storms and I prayed she wouldn't cry again. The thunder boomed loudly, the room shaking each time it happened. Jo kept her head covered the entire time the storm was doing its thing in the large, dark sky.

Then it became a muted sound that I could scarcely hear. At that very moment, rain started coming down in sheets so that I couldn't see beyond the windows. It was making me want to go home and get in my own bed. But, I didn't have my bed anymore. I was on a high bed that wasn't big enough for two people and it wasn't in my home.

Then Jo started crying. She wouldn't stop and I finally got the nerves to find my way to the front office where the woman with white hair was reading.

She looked up from the book and frowned at me. "What are you doing up, Shelby?"

"Can my sister get in bed with me? She's scared of the thundering and lightning. We always sleep together at home."

"You best get used to sleeping alone, young lady. After this week you won't be living together. You'll go to one house and your sister will go to another one," the woman said.

"Why can't we sleep together? Why are you so mean to us? What have we done to make you dislike us?" She was rejecting us just like Papa had. And I knew she would never love us.

"I would advise you to get in bed and go to sleep. Stop getting up and asking me questions, there is nothing I can do, young lady."

I ran back to the bedroom and crawled up on the high bed I was told to sleep in. I thought about what the woman with the white hair told me. Why would anyone separate us? Evidently, she knew what she was talking about, but I didn't grasp it. She was not an unbearable person, but she made sure I understood where she was coming from.

It took some time for me to get to sleep, but it wasn't long before I was dreaming and someone telling me that I would always live here and I would never see my family of genes again. Jo and I didn't recognize love for many years to come. We were alone, two small children, ages eight and seven, to take care of ourselves from here on out.

Eight

IF WE COULD run away, where would we sleep? If we didn't have food, what would we eat? All these things I pondered while trying to go to sleep. We couldn't live by ourselves because we were too young. We had to take a deep breath and start living in a place we didn't know.

I knew my sister loved me even at the age of seven. She even told me that at times. I loved her unconditionally and still do. Even when she wouldn't go with me to a member of our daddy's family, I loved her and knew she was shy at that time in her life. We loved one another even when we disagree. That love never leaves because our love is unconditional, forever.

Jo is more like our daddy in looks, whereas I look and act more like our mother, wanting to be doing something constantly. Jo can sit and watch television and she is a much calmer lady while I'm not like that at all. I happen to be a person who doesn't care to sit around for long periods of time—I want to be moving, doing something. It works on my brain when I try to sit and do absolutely nothing. I want to scream out due to the nervousness I feel with nothing to do.

Sitting . . . doing nothing . . . not in my makeup. I need to keep my brain working on projects all the time. My brain runs a mile a second when not doing something productive. If I am sitting, I am reading, crocheting, or sewing.

I am sure I have attention-deficit/hyperactivity disorder (ADHD). A friend of mine told me this a few years ago, when we were cooking for our church's dinner on Wonderful Wednesday nights. Since she had her doctorate in education, I'm sure she knew what she was talking about since she sees children like me all the time. I had to agree with her because it's true.

THE NEXT MORNING I woke to the loud sound of a bell ringing. It echoed in my ears, scaring me to the point of screaming out loud. I jumped up and looked out the window. Then I ran to the end of the bedroom and looked in a different direction. It kept ringing and it startled me. I couldn't see the bell that was ringing and I figured it was going to ring all the time. It isn't that loud when you get used to hearing it, but this morning it was extremely loud. The bell made me nervous. I didn't know what I would be facing today.

A girl came to the bedroom and told us it was time to get up. She told us to get dressed, wash our face, brush our teeth, and get to the dining room, pronto. We got up and put the same clothes on we had worn yesterday and did as we were told.

We both had long hair. Jo's hair was slightly wavy whereas my hair was curly, curly, tight curls that stuck out slightly from my head. My curly hair was brushed until it shined. My teeth were unbelievable white from where I brushed them so long. I wanted to do what the girl said so no one would fuss at Jo or me.

I loved my new dress, it was a beautiful shade of blue and so pretty. Our married aunt had taken us shopping for new clothes in Raleigh. Papa gave her the money for the things we would need. I even had new shoes and socks to wear to my new home. I wondered if I would stay here forever or if we would be shipped off again.

We had forgotten where the dining room was. The night before, we went to the kitchen to eat. Maybe we should try to find the kitchen. I thought about the playroom and where we went for supper. I knew the kitchen was just a short distant from where we were standing last night. The house was larger than my school, a huge building.

Jo Ann and I did as we were told and walked down that long, desolate hallway to the kitchen, our shoes making squeaking noise as we walked. It hadn't been hard to find after all. I remembered where the playroom was, so I followed the long hallway to it.

There was the same older lady and girl cooking. The lady told us to sit down and she would feed us in the kitchen. She was very nice and so was the girl. We had eggs and bacon, along with toast.

After I finished eating all I wanted, I was told I had to eat all of the breakfast. I had eaten everything except the toast. We had no jelly and I didn't want plain toast. If I had jelly to make the toast slide down easily, I would like it much better.

"Shelby, you have to eat your toast. Put some molasses on it and it will taste good," the teenager said. Then she sat down next to me and showed me how to do it. "You will get used to it because we have it every morning of the week. After you have eaten it a few times you're going to love it."

I thought, *Are you crazy?*

I did as I was told and but it was so terrible. It stuck to the roof of my mouth, causing me to gag and drink plenty of milk. I had never eaten molasses before and it just wasn't good. What made that girl say I would learn to love it? I would never learn to like this black, sweet, thick stuff. However, she had a good laugh when I was gagging. That caused Jo to smile at her.

While I was gagging the woman said, "You don't have to eat your toast with the molasses. I can see that you have never had it."

I was a happy camper then. Jo Ann was crying because she didn't care for it either. The woman opened the refrigerator and got out some apple jelly for us to smear on our toast.

Jo and I had learned that this was the infirmary and Mrs. Tomblin was the nurse. We spent days in there I think, but for the life of me I can't remember what we did. I know we had shots and our head was looked over that first morning to see if we had lice. Mrs. Tomblin took us to the basement and told us to bend over the table where she put a towel. She then picked up a fine tooth comb and started combing my hair. It was a funny looking comb, one I had never seen before. A teenage girl did the same thing to Jo Ann. We both were scared to death being in the basement. We didn't understand why she was combing our hair when we had already combed it before breakfast.

The basement at the infirmary was a dark, spooky place except where we were standing. It was almost as large as the top floors. There were lights in the room but it was still a scary place to be. I got used to it when I was a teenager when I worked at the infirmary with Mrs. Tomblin. If I can recall, all the rooms seem to have sinks in them. It looked like it was used for that purpose during the war to treat soldiers. Now that I think of it, it could have been used for that purpose way back in the early years in World War One.

We didn't have lice so Mrs. Tomblin didn't have to cut our hair. We were able to go upstairs to the playroom. Several teenage girls came by and spoke to us. They were very nice and pleased we weren't crying anymore. I guess we played with the toys or picked up a book to look at or read.

I don't remember what we did or how long we stayed with Mrs. Tomblin. After the traumatized feeling of being left with this woman, I'm not sure how long we stayed. It could have only been a few days. I was so disheartened and sad because we had done something to make Papa dislike us. Of course, we probably made him mad when we wanted to come home from his sister-in-law's house, but he didn't seem to stay mad. I figured it would be the same this time.

Time must have gone by fast because I don't remember anything we did except going to another building to be fitted with clothes. We couldn't keep all the clothes we had, and I was in tears when we were taken back to the infirmary. They had given us someone's clothes that were not new like ours. Every girl had an allotted amount of clothes to wear each day. What would they do with our new clothes? Would they throw them away or give them to someone else?

That same day we were taken to the shoe shop for shoes. We had one pair to wear during the week and one pair for

Sunday. We kept the shoes Papa had bought for us to wear on Sunday. Our own shoes were getting too small so the old man with gray hair fitted us with another pair to be worn during the week. I didn't care for the old man because he kept putting his hand around my waist, causing me to have to stand there. Jo and the teenage girl sat on the bench and didn't pay any attention to the old man.

We were beginning to know the routine at the infirmary. That loud bell woke us each morning at six o'clock. It was close by and the sound still penetrated our small brains, causing us to jump up out of our bed like someone was after us.

Each morning some of the boys and girls came to the infirmary to be treated by Mrs. Tomblin. These were the children that had colds or cuts. She treated each one and sent them on their way. It was nice to see them walking down to the infirmary because we knew there were more children than we knew about.

One morning Mrs. Tomblin called us to the living room. We were going to a cottage where other girls lived. What a happy day I was going to have. Mrs. Tomblin became nicer and we finally were somewhat enjoying ourselves.

The bedroom at the infirmary had a few girls because they were sick. They were not allowed to get out of the bed except to go to the bathroom. One girl was really sick, but the others didn't seem to be sick at all. They talked to us and told us what to expect once we left. They were the ages of Jo and me. One of the girls said I would go to the same cottage she was at. Her name was Patty Jo. I couldn't remember her last name.

There was also another large bedroom across the short hallway from where we were sleeping. I learned it was for boys who were sick. It looked the same as the girls' bedroom. I even saw some boys in there when I went exploring. I didn't understand why there were so many beds on both sides.

The next day a teenager came to the infirmary to take us to our new home. Jo Ann went to the baby cottage and I went to the Royster Building. We looked at one another and started crying again. We had never been separated.

I had always been told to look after my younger sister. Knowing we would not be living together tore my heart out. Didn't they let brothers and sisters stay together? We were the new kids on the block and hadn't done anything, so why were they separating me from my sister?

Nine

THERE WERE AROUND twenty-five girls in my cottage. I got to know them fast, some I didn't care for. Two teenage girls stayed in the house with us. Since Jo was in the Baby Cottage, she had to obey the ones in charge there. I couldn't understand why she went to a baby cottage because she wasn't a baby. I have never understood the irony of this. She was seven years old and should have been in the Royster Building with me.

The bedroom was like the one at the infirmary. There were at least twenty-five white iron beds for the girls who lived there. These beds were not high as the ones in the infirmary. They were low enough for the smallest person to get on.

The teenage girls who stayed in the Royster Building were Helen and Bobbie. The counselor of the cottage was Mrs. Womblin. I didn't know what a counselor was supposed to be, but it didn't take me long to find out. I didn't like her as soon as I was introduced to her. She never smiled.

Counselor was a new word for me. I was learning things at a fast pace, educating myself to the ways of my new home. I knew she was not the kindest person in the world. She held her hands funny when she walked, opening and closing them quite often. It seemed to me that she was angry all the time for some odd reason.

That first morning after moving in, she gave me a chore to do. I had to clean the floor registers where the heat came from, getting all the dust from them. It wasn't wintertime, it was spring and the heat wasn't on that much as I remembered. I cleaned those registers every day regardless, even in the summertime. There were a lot of them to clean. I tried hard to get them done and be ready to walk to the dining room for breakfast each day. I didn't have chores at home, only when we were staying with Papa's sister-in-law.

I had to make my bed as soon as I hit the floor each morning and there could not be any wrinkles in it. It wasn't too hard, and Helen showed me how to make the corners right. This was something she said I had to do it every morning. We were never allowed to ever sleep late, regardless of how we felt. I liked Helen that first day and she had the prettiest smile. She became a good friend after she left our orphanage home.

That week was a long one. Mrs. Womblin was unpleasant to all the girls and I was terrified when she walked into the room. She had her own room and we were not allowed to enter unless we were going to be scolded. I was told I had to be quiet, not loud at any time. Hey, I was a child and couldn't stay quiet all the time. I wanted to talk to the other girls so I would get to know them. If we were so quiet, how could we become friends?

SINCE IT WAS April when Jo and I got to the orphanage, we had to go to school the second or third day after being dropped off the planet. The school was close to the infirmary, it didn't take long to walk there. I don't remember who took us to school that first day. I do remember seeing lots of boys and girls in my class. Living in the Royster Building was the longest walk from the school and we had to walk and carry our books. Not that we had that many, but I didn't care to carry them in my arms. We finally got a homemade book sack that we used for all of our books.

I even got to go to the library to check out a book to read in the cottage. When I first walked into the library and saw all those books on different shelves I was in hog's heaven. I was learning to read fast and I could hardly wait to pick out a book. My first day in the library I fanned the books and smelled them and that's still something I still do when I pick up a book to read. I love the smell of books when I open them, whether they are new or old. When I am reading I forget everything except what's in the book.

I was nearing the end of the third grade and my teacher's name was Miss Simpson. I will never forget her because she called me to her desk that first week and asked me to spell a word. I tried hard to spell it. I can't remember what the word was but I was petrified then.

I turned around and saw a big smile on a boy's face and that caused me to stutter. I was scared out of my wits and nervous due to the other students staring and smiling at me. Why were they smiling at me, was I that bad at spelling?

Stuttering had never happened to me before. My unmarried uncle stuttered and now I was like him. I couldn't get the word out and I tried so hard. I got teary-eyed. Those students kept looking at me and smiling and I wanted to tell them to stop.

Why couldn't I get the word out of my mouth and spell it. I knew how to spell it but those eyes were observing . . . watching . . . waiting . . . seeing what I would do next. Being the new kid, I didn't know the rules Miss Simpson expected of me.

They knew I didn't know what to expect. She pinched me under my arm, where the skin is thin and sensitive, and kept pinching me to make me spell the word. If I didn't spell it correctly, she pinched me again. How can anyone spell if you know someone is going to keep pinching you?

I learned that first day in my new school what Miss Simpson expected of me. That day I started stuttering, not as bad as my uncle, but I was doing the same thing. I remember the words starting with "S" or "M" were hard to say and I stuttered trying to get the word out. I stuttered for a few years and then it left. I'm sure it was related to stress.

From that day on I learned to spell all the words. We didn't use phonics back then, but I think I'm a pretty good speller most of the time. Using computers makes it much easier because some of the time the computer realizes the word and will finish spelling it for you.

IT TOOK A long time to adjust to orphanage life. I missed my family so much and wanted to see them. I didn't hear from anyone and I finally got used to living with a lot of girls. Some of them were nice, but some were not. It didn't matter one way or the other. I had to take a deep breath, suck it up, smile, and go about my business of being a good girl.

One morning when I was going back to the Royster Building, after breakfast, I saw the superintendent, Mr. Proctor, coming toward me. He was a big man and had the biggest hands I had ever seen. Even his shoes were big and long. He stopped me and asked me what my name was and how I was doing. I told him my name while looking way up to see his face. He was a very tall man—at least he was to a small child. He then he patted me on the head and it was an expression of love to me.

I remember saying, "The war is over, I just heard about it."

He smiled and asked me, "Who told you the war was over?"

Looking way up and smiling at this big man, I said, "I heard Mrs. Womblin telling Helen and Bobbie."

He smiled and told me I was a smart little girl. Then he patted me on the head again and told me to get on so I wouldn't get in trouble. That was the only time I saw the man that I remember. I think he retired shortly after that day. It's strange how we can remember certain aspects of life and then no recollection of some of the larger parts.

Some of the girls tried to take advantage of me, wanting me to do things for them. If I didn't do what they wanted, they would tell on me for some reason. I seemed to get in a lot of trouble that year. Now that I was learning the ins and outs of orphanage life, I learned not listen to the girls wanting me to do something bad for them. I would turn around and walk away. This worked for me the entire time I was there.

On Saturday mornings we met in the study hall/play room for an hour to memorize the little book that Helen and Bobbie had. Some of the questions were, "Who is God, who is Jesus, and who was Moses." I tried my best to remember all the questions because we had to repeat them the next Saturday morning. I think the little book was called the catechism.

This was unusual for me because I had learned most of these things in Sunday school. I was used to going to church on Sunday and loved it when I was at home. Saturday mornings I didn't care for, especially after breakfast, learning that little book. I wanted to go outside and play since we didn't have to go to school.

There was one girl who beat her head on the bed frame every night to go to sleep. I slept next to her and had to listen to this night after night for at least a year. No one could keep her from beating the crap out of her head. I tried doing the same thing once and it hurt so bad, I stopped. I figured she was so used to it and it didn't hurt anymore. Her name was Carolyn Caldwell and she ended up being a friend of mine for the rest of her years in our orphanage home.

I remember Carolyn couldn't swim and they tried numerous times to help her. Miss Pender was the high school P.E. teacher and she was in charge of making sure we learned to swim in the summer. She got so mad at Carolyn because she wouldn't try to swim. Carolyn was terrified of the water, and when they pushed her off the diving board, she sunk to the bottom of the pool.

All the girls knew Carolyn would never learn to swim since she was so terrified of the water. One day Miss Pender kept her in the pool for four hours. She was in that pool with the large boys who swam from three to four as I remember. Carolyn was crying and being bullied beyond reasoning. Even today, I don't know if Carolyn ever learned to swim or not. Some people just can't do it or they become horrified of being in the deep end of a pool. I hated that woman for bullying Carolyn.

It was not fair to take a young child and abuse her that way. Miss Pender became my enemy from that day on. She was unkind to Carolyn and several of us hated her for treating Carolyn so bad.

Ten

WE HEARD THAT bell ring every *morning* to wake us up. That same bell rang to go to the dining room three times a day. Then the stupid bell rang walk to school on campus. That stupid bell kept ringing different times of the day, every day. Ding dong . . . ding dong . . . ding dong. Never did it not clang for us to get somewhere on campus daily. It became a habit listening for that stupid bell telling me what to do, where to go, controlling my life constantly.

I looked forward to it when it was time to eat. I ate in the basement of the dining room when I first went to the orphanage. I had to sit at a table with five other children. We didn't have snacks after school like Jo and I had at home. We had three large meals a day and nothing in between. There were not many fat students at the orphanage, either. We worked the fat off at our jobs when we were not in school.

I remember Steven Dean sat at my table. I was shy, and he would smile at me and I would blush. He didn't care for cabbage and wouldn't eat it. He would stuff it in his jacket pocket and throw it away once he left the dining room. The woman in charge saw him do this one night at dinner and made him stand up and eat all the cabbage out of his pocket.

It was embarrassing for us having to watch him eat that cabbage. I believe this to be a form of abuse. I'm sure my mouth was wide opened the entire time he was trying to eat all that cabbage plus the dirt in his pocket.

I made sure to eat everything on my plate and not throw any away. I would push it around my plate so it wasn't so noticeable. I didn't like the scrambled eggs we were served just about every day. As I look back, I don't think we ever had fried eggs. It would take entirely too long to cook fried eggs for all the orphans and teachers.

I would wash those scrambled eggs down with my milk, but there was never any left on my plate. I didn't want to have to stand up and eat the eggs while all the rest of the boys and girls looked at me and snickered. We got a boiled egg on Wednesday and Sunday mornings, which I loved. I love eggs cooked different ways now that I am a grown woman. In fact, I love them for dinner at times. My favorite way of cooking them is to poach them. No one else in my family cares for them this way, but to me they are the best. I even love scrambled eggs a lot.

I was told that first day that I had to eat everything on my plate. I couldn't ask for seconds even when I loved what I was eating. Every Saturday night we had hot dogs on a bun with beans and cold slaw. I guess that's the reason I love hot dogs today.

On Wednesday and Sunday nights we had sandwiches for dinner. The sandwiches were peanut butter and molasses. I didn't like them at first as I have already stated, but it didn't take me long to look forward to a peanut butter and molasses sandwich. Today they are undeniably the best thing in the world. Even my husband likes a peanut butter molasses sandwich once in a while for lunch.

A lot of Wednesdays, we had chicken and dumplings at lunch versus a sandwich because we had sandwiches on Wednesday nights. On Sunday for lunch we always had fried chicken and it was the best fried chicken I have ever eaten. I loved the way it was cooked, and when I worked in the kitchen I was the one who helped fry it every other Sunday when I had to work and not go to church.

We always had a mixture of meat, starches, and veggies. On Wednesday and Sunday nights we normally got a piece of fruit like an orange, apple, or banana with the sandwiches. My favorite was the orange. Some of the boys would ask for my fruit, but no one was going to get my fruit from me. I was a fruit lover then and still am today. I normally have an orange, banana, or apple every day.

Sometimes for lunch we had a sandwich of potted ham or spam, something of that nature. It was really good with lots of mustard and mayonnaise. It came in a long tin and the girls in the kitchen sliced it for the lunch meal. I haven't had that since leaving my orphanage home. I probably would still like it. In fact, I can almost taste the potted meat we had sixty years ago.

We had wonderful food just about every day. I was not a finicky eater, having learned to eat all foods at Papa's home. I still enjoy vegetables versus the meats. Now of course, I like meats but I can go without them.

We even had an ice cream machine. On Sundays we got some sort of desert to go with the ice cream. Mr. Pruitt was in charge of the food and was the dietitian as long as I lived at my orphanage home. When I was in the eleventh grade, he caught us kitchen girls enjoying the ice cream in the freezer. He kept it locked but we knew where the key hung on a nail.

He wasn't married when he first came to work at our home. I think he had just gotten out of the army and this was his first job after fighting for our country. Time passed and he was dating one of the women who worked in Ole Gray's office. I think she was Ole Gray's secretary. They were finally married and were one of the happiest couples I've ever known. Of course, I didn't know whether they fussed or not. I liked Mr. Pruitt; he seemed to be shy, but when he smiled, you knew he liked you.

Ole Gray was the superintendent of the orphanage. His name was A. De Leon Gray. All the children called him Ole Gray for some reason. He came to the orphanage soon after I arrived and was still there when I left.

I HAD A hard time adjusting to my new life. One morning I was in the bathroom, sitting on the toilet, peeing. Being curious about my body I wanted to find out where the pee came from. I turned around and tried to see, but since I couldn't see from the back, I opened my legs and tried to see from the front. The stalls had doors on them, but anyone could open the stall door while you were doing your personal business. There was no way to lock the door to keep anyone from entering the booth with you.

Well, I was trying my best to look and that stall opened so fast my heart stopped beating for a second. All I could see were some large feet. Then I looked up and there was Bobbie with her hands on her hips, staring at me with a sour look on her face. Then she frowned.

She had a sneer on her face and yelled, "What are you looking at, Shelby?"

"Nothing." I didn't want her to know I was curious about my body.

"Stop looking at yourself, get through peeing, there are others who need to use the toilet. You are such a dirty girl, watching yourself pee while going to the bathroom." She then stood there and waited for me to finish. "You are such a dirty girl. Why do you do things like this, sexual things?"

I didn't say anything, I didn't know what sexual things she was talking about. I didn't even know what that word *sexual* meant. I thought I had done something ugly. It left me feeling uncomfortable throughout my years in my orphanage home. I would never say such a thing to anyone, nor would I stand there and watch. After all, your body belongs to you and you have the right to look at it.

Episodes like this made me feel dirty and it lasted until after I graduated. Each time Bobbie would say something to me I would cringe and not look her in the eye. As long as she was in the Royster Building, I could never look her in the eye again. From that day on I never looked to see what any part of my body looked like. I still feel guilty thinking about it.

Even when I began to grow in the breast area, I never stood at the sink to see how much I had grown. I knew I would have to start wearing bras, but I didn't want to until I was a lot older. All the girls said they were uncomfortable.

I never looked to see if I was growing pubic hair. Today I talk to my granddaughters about their bodies and tell them that their body is a blessing from God and it's theirs. I also tell them it is not a sin to look at yourself in the mirror to see where you are growing.

Bobbie didn't like me, nor did she like most of the girls. Perhaps she didn't care for herself. Her mother was a counselor for the large boys' cottage, called the 4-B at a later date. I think Bobbie had graduated from high school when her mother came to the orphanage to work.

Even her brother became the 4-B counselor when I was a teenager. The boys didn't care for him at all. They all said he was odd and sexual mistreated some of the boys. Most of the time he got away with handling the boys in a bad way, but some never let him touch them. I don't know if he grew up in our orphanage home or not.

While living in the Royster Building, we had to pick up acorns that dropped from the huge, one-hundred-year-old oak trees during the winter months. We used a gallon can to put them in. We got one-half penny for each can we picked up. This kept us out of trouble and we didn't work very hard picking them up. There were more acorns on campus than anyone could imagine because oak trees were everywhere, especially on the front lawn where the cottages were.

Today I love those beautiful, old, oak trees, they are huge now. I love sitting under them and talking to some of my brothers or sisters. Some of the trees were destroyed when hurricane Hazel came through, but there are still a lot of them on the campus. When I was a teenager, we were allowed to congregate on the main road on Sunday afternoon. We would sit under those oak trees and talk. Some of the time the boys would wander over to spend time with us. It was nice being with the boys when we were in the 4-G cottage. There were benches on both side of the road where we could also sit and talk. We enjoyed our Sunday afternoons whether there were boys or not.

Eleven

WHILE I WAS still in the Royster Building I had to walk to the shoe shop for shoes. Several times I had to go alone because none of the other girls needed larger shoes or they were working at their job. I had outgrown mine, according to Mrs. Womblin. I was taken in the room that held all the shoes, girls and boys together. The smallest to the largest sizes were lined up on the shelves.

The man in charge of the shoe department pulled me over to him and told me I could have any shoes I wanted if they fitted me. While he was holding me around the waist so I couldn't get free, he slid his other hand under my dress and pulled my panties aside and I didn't know what to do. He then used me in my most private place and it began to alarm me. No one had ever done this to me before and I didn't know what to do. I was frightened beyond words and didn't know why he was doing it. He used his finger to hurt me and cause me to cry out.

Tears flowed from my eyes while he kept doing it. I didn't know what it was called, but I knew it was wicked. What had I done to make him use my body this way? I was humiliated, horrified, and I felt soiled and filthy, causing me to cry more. He kept it up until one of the boys, who worked at the shoe shop, came in. I was being punished for something I had done. That was why Papa left me here for this man to use me for his enjoyment. My heart was beating fast because I was being penalized for some reason.

He finished abusing me and gave me the shoes I needed and then told me to leave. I never told anyone what had happened. I didn't know what to say or how to tell anyone about the episodes. They would think I was dirty again . . . and . . . again. Bobbie would yell at me and then Miss Womblin would punish me for telling a lie. I was beginning to know the ends and outs of my new home real fast.

No one would believe this nice old gentleman would sexually abuse a child in my orphanage home. Yeah, right. He had the perfect place to do it because he knew no one would tell on him. He grew up in my orphanage home and probably knew he could get away it. I know he was married and lived in Oxford. He had children and probably grandchildren my age. He was a bastard and I still hate him today for using my small body to fill his sexual urges.

Several times this happened to me. I hated going alone, petrified to walk down that long sidewalk to the shoe shop. It wasn't far from the Royster Building and it only took a short time to get there, but for me it was a long way. I knew that old man was going to do things to me again.

I finally asked Miss Womblin if someone could go with me to the shoe shop to be fitted with larger shoes. I was in tears when I asked her and I think she recognized what was happening and let someone go with me. If I had said anything, grown-ups would say I had a dirty mind, just like Bobbie said to me.

A problem like this for a child is a horrifying awareness of knowing you are a nasty, filthy, and a disgusting human being. It was so horrible that I tried to hide it and not let anyone know my panties had a small amount of blood on them when I went to the bathroom. I managed to wash them in the toilet while alone in the bathroom. Then I put them back on to dry. It upset me so much that I cried as I washed my panties, hoping no one would see or hear me. However, no one could see or hear me unless they opened that stall door. It left me with a frightening nightmare of being used over . . . and . . . over . . . again.

I am in tears reliving what the old man did to me when I took that long walk to the shoe shop, scared to death.

"Why did this have to happen to me as such a young age? Where were the people who were supposed to protect me?"

No child should have to experience this behavior from men. It's sickening to say the least. Writing about it gives me that same repulsive feeling I had then. It makes me feel degraded, tainted, and unworthy to others. This should never happen to a child. They don't know whether it's a bad or wicked thing.

I have always said no man better not touch my daughters in the way I was touched. I would buy a gun and kill them. I am sure that I would be in prison now if that had happened. Now I say the same about my granddaughters.

I never mentioned this to anyone until I was in my forties. I figured by that time no one would call me a dirty old woman. I'm sure I'm not the only one he sexually abused.

LESS THAN A year in my new home, Papa came to see us during the Thanksgiving holiday, which was a big surprise for Jo and me. I was in the infirmary due to a virus I had picked up. I was in the first bed in the dormitory on the right as you entered it. Jo was with Papa and a woman. Papa said hello and told me she was my new grandmother. He had brought our Christmas gifts with them so they didn't have to come back for any reason.

I remember I got a book of different places in the United States and when I opened the book parts stood up. It was called a *Jolly Jump Up* book. For instance, Washington, D.C. the White House, and Washington Monument stood up with several other things. It also had the Grand Canyon in it.

I still have this book. I will pass it on down to my grandchildren to give to their children one day. It's in bad shape and I had it hanging on the wall for a few years. I might get it glued and bound again so it won't tear any more. This was the only gift from Papa I received other than the stretchable bracelet.

I was to call this woman grandmother which I never did. When I saw her, I called her by her given name or I didn't call her anything. I never thought of her as a grandmother. She came to Papa's and with her came two daughters and one granddaughter. They didn't work, they stayed home or rode up and down the road doing their own thing. They certainly didn't help barn tobacco or pick cotton. They were living like queens while my unmarried aunt worked in the fields and became their personal maid.

They took over the house and my unmarried aunt became the one to do the washing and house cleaning. She was never a daughter to the woman. As I write this I cannot, for the life of me, feel good about that woman and her girls. My unmarried aunt and uncle had a new mother who didn't care for them at all. In fact, I don't think Papa brought her home until after they were married. So this woman was a surprise to all my mother's family.

They lived this way until Papa's new wife finally left him before he died at the age of ninety. I guess she had gotten everything she could out of the marriage. There wasn't anything else she could get from him. It could have been Papa who had enough of her and her family. I never heard why she left, maybe because Papa was old and couldn't remember things. She was a lot younger. Both her daughters and grandchild left several years before the step-grandmother.

Twelve

I STAYED OUT of trouble and made friends in the Royster Building as I moved forward to the next cottage. One of girls I was friends with was Mozilla Kirkindoft. She and I hit it off at once. She had been there since she was a baby. She was a little thing as I remember but we were the same age. She could get on the high diving board at the swimming pool and make the prettiest dive I've ever seen. She could've made the Olympics had she entered. She and I found so much to do together. We worked together when we were teenagers in the kitchen and the dining rooms.

THE ORPHANAGE WAS split into two different sections. The girls were on the right side and the boys were on the left side as you entered the main road. We didn't dare step beyond our territory. Stepping over the invisible line was a no-no. The only day we could cross over was Sunday afternoon when we were a junior or senior. We could stay outside then and talk to the boys whether it was a hot summer day or a cold, rainy, or snow day. This was our day to get together with our boyfriend at the beginning of a new week. This was only for the boys and girls in the 4-B and 4-G. We had to be teenagers to get this privilege.

MY LIFE IN the Royster Building was my first entrance to the ways of my orphanage home. Mrs. Womblin walked with authority and everyone got out of her way when she came around. I lived in the Royster Building for two years and then I was sent to the 1-G, (first girl's cottage) where Miss King was the cottage counselor.

What can I say about Miss King? How do I tell you about this lady who was an old maid? Not only was she was an old maid, but she acted the part. Her hair was thin and she pulled it back in a knot at the back of her head. I can't remember anyone liking this woman.

We were always saying the orphanage was the place for old maids to end up. Why they were chosen to be the one to teach us was very misleading. If the truth was known then, we could have taught those old maids about life. All the girls made fun of her when she had her back turned to us. We snickered and held back the giggle that wanted to escape.

She had this little high-pitched bell she rang when it was time to come in from outside. Every day she rang that stupid bell. As if we didn't have enough bells ringing . . . every . . . single day. Oh well, we got used to hearing this bell loud and clear. It had a much higher pitch than the one that rang ding-dong telling us where to head out each day. How we hated that little bell ringing and some of us would tarry just because she was ringing it. We would slowly get up from the ground and dillydally before going in the house. The pitch was so high, it hurt my ears if I was anywhere close to her.

I found my best friend, Mary Janice Moore, in the 1-G cottage. We did just about everything together. She and her sister, Betty Jean, came after I was already there. She was a lot shorter than me and I called her little bit most of the time. It was hard for her to lose the weight she carried throughout her life. Though she was on the hefty side, she was beautiful to me. I loved this woman as a sister and I still get tears when talking about her. She already had two sisters living in our home. They were Weta and Ida. Janice and Betty Jean came a few years later.

When we finished our work we would go outside to spend time before Miss King rang that stupid earsplitting bell for us to come inside. When it was summertime we would lay on the alfalfa field and look for four-leaf clovers to make a wish. We knew it would come true and we would find our prince charming. Of course, it never came true, but we looked for them regardless and hoped that wish would come true one day.

When you wish for something you were supposed to keep it a secret but Janice and I always told each other. We weren't very serious because we knew it would never come true. Day dreaming was relaxing and we did it when we looked for that lucky four-leaf clover.

Most of the time we would wish for a certain boy to like us. There were different boys we liked, but we didn't expose this to the other girls. If we had, they would go and tell the boy. Then we would be too shy to speak to him. This happened time and time again to me during my years of orphanage life. I wasn't shy but I didn't want any boy to know I had a crush on him.

Janice and I would lay on the ground and look up at the clouds in the sky. If it was a sunny day, the clouds moved slowly across that big blue sky. As they moved over, others would take their place. Janice and I would make different things from those beautiful clouds. I still remember the good times we had when we dreamed of larger and better things that we would have when we became adults. She always wanted to teach school and I always wanted to be a nurse like Florence Nightingale or Claire Barton.

It was so much fun to lay there and see which cloud we could find a dog, cat, or angel. We made animals from the clouds all the time. Once in a while we would see a big face and we would say it was God's face looking down on us. We even made trees and bushes from those clouds. Sometime we could actually see angels with wings floating around in the clouds. We knew God was looking after us and we thanked Him for letting us see angels with their headpiece of gold that was lit up like a star when the sun was bright on our angel.

Those day are precious to me as I sit here writing about my life with my handpicked family of three-hundred-and-twenty some children. Life is good when you have as many brothers and sisters as I do. I sit here and smile while I'm typing as fast as I can so I don't forget to tell something that pops in my head. I can't contain the joy I feel when I think of these wonderful people that came into my life by no fault of their own.

My family of orphans are dear to me and I love hearing about them, what they are doing, how many children they have, plus grandchildren. There are so many it's hard to remember everything about them. When I see that smile on a face of one them, my love for them is full and I want to hug and kiss them and tell them I love them to the moon and back. They make my day pleasant when I think of them.

We are alike in so many ways, but still different. The happiness we have for each other is one hundred percent all the time. As of today I can't wait to return home to see some of my orphan family I love. They make me content and tranquil because these orphans are my handpicked family.

Recalling those days of long ago gives me a genuine feeling throughout my body, almost triggering my heart to overflow with the love I have for my orphanage home. It became a place where I never got bored. It was a happy place when we were together as children, then teenagers, then adults. Not a worry in the world, going about our days as a happy camper.

While lying on the alfalfa field one day Janice and I made up a song about Miss King and her piercing bell. We finally got it down pat and it goes like this:

> *When the sun is setting in the evenings*
> *And Ms. King gets out her cow bell*
> *She will call the 1-G cows from the pasture*
> *To get ready for the hay.*
> *Get along home 1-G cows,*
> *get along home 1-G cows,*
> *and get along home 1-G cows*
> *Get ready for grub.*

I still remember that song and it makes me smile because Janice died around 2009. We sang this song the last time I saw her at the rehabilitation center in Mount Olive, North Carolina. Oh yeah, she was my best friend even after she died. She was a wonderful wife, mother, and teacher. Her students loved her because she was soft spoken and never yelled at them. She was good to the students she had every year until she retired from being a great teacher.

One afternoon, right before the dinner hour, someone mentioned something about a convict hanging around my orphanage home. It scared us so bad we were petrified. Janice and I took a case knife from our table and hid it somewhere in our clothing before we left the dining room. It must have been during winter months because we had coats to hide those knives. We took ours back to the 1-G cottage and hid them under our bed covers. I knew that man was going to come to kill some of the girls and I wanted to be prepared. I slept with that knife for days until I didn't hear anything else about the convict. Sometime later I took it from my jacket pocket and laid it on the table at dinner time. Maybe there was a convict around my home but he never ended up in one of the cottages.

Twelve

DURING THE TIME I was in 1-G we had jobs outside the cottage. I started working in the vegetable house. In the summer months we would prepare fresh vegetables for meals. The boys picked the vegetables from the field and brought them to the vegetable house. We girls shelled butter beans and peas during the time we were there to work. During that time we did a lot of talking. The vegetables were so good when they were cooked and sitting on my plate waiting for me to dig in.

There were two or three large girls to oversee us. Julia Fitchett was the one I enjoyed talking to the most. She had the longest nails I had ever seen and they were so hard. She taught me how to crochet and knit. I could only do a few things but those things came back to me once I started crocheting a few years ago. I now make my own sweaters.

I saw her not too many years ago at homecoming and she didn't recognize me. I ran up to her and told her my name. She grabbed me and we started hugging and kissing each other. I reminded her of how I loved to feel her nails because they were so long and hard. It was the only time I ever saw Julia. As far as I know, she has gone on to Heaven to be with other orphan brothers and sisters.

At some time, when I was a high school girl, we had a chicken coup with lots of chickens. The vegetable house was used to clean chickens when they were ready to be killed. I don't remember if they were frozen after we finished cleaning and cutting them up. I'm pretty sure they were frozen for later use because there were so many of them. Those days we didn't go to school. We had to get up and head out to the vegetable house after breakfast to start our day of chicken cleaning.

We would dip that dead chicken in scalding water to help remove the feathers. Then we would start picking the feathers off. After that we cut them open to remove the insides and a lot of the time there were eggs forming. I didn't particular like doing this, but it was my job. There was a foul-smelling odor all around us as we cleaned those nasty chickens. If you have ever smelled wet feathers, you know what I mean. Greasy hands, aprons wet and greasy, and we smelled like those wet chickens we were cleaning.

The vegetable house would smell of wet chickens for days. I thought, after I had cleaned them for days, I would never eat chicken again. But I loved it so much I forgot about the smell and cleaning them. My orphan sister, Mary Willis Merrill, still can't stand to eat chicken. She informed me she smells the vegetable house every time she sees fried chicken. I should say any kind of chicken.

However, I learned to cut a chicken up and still do it today. I taught my daughters how to cut them in different parts but they buy the separate pieces that are already cut up. Today whole chicken are not seen in the meat section as much. At certain times the stores sell whole chickens and I will buy them and make chicken and pastry from them.

It was that way for a lot of the girls, but lordy, lordy, I do love fried chicken and chicken and pastry. I can't go long before I have to cook my favorite meat, chicken in any form. Sorry, Mary, I have forgotten the terrible smell and I do love my fried chicken like we made in the kitchen at our orphanage home.

LIFE WAS GOOD because I was not one for getting in trouble. I behaved and did as I was told just about all the time. When my sister was in the Baby Cottage I would only see her when I went to the dining room for meals. I couldn't spend time with her, but I would wave to her when I saw the smaller ones outside the Baby Cottage. She always looked so sad and of course I was sad too, yet I couldn't run over and give her a hug and kiss. We just stayed where we were and waved. It was miserable to see her this way, but there was nothing I could do. She was so small in my eyes and her eyes didn't shine the way

I remembered before coming to the orphanage. Her little arms kept waving until I had to go in the dining room.

My heart ached to spend time with her but that was a no-no. It became normal for me to wave and then go about my business. If I had tried to spend time with her, I would get in trouble and that would mean a spanking or some sort of punishment.

Children would come to the orphanage at different times of the year. Just about every few months there would be new children arriving. It was nice when girls my age arrived and we became friends. Not every girl in the cottage was a friend of mine. I knew them, but we didn't play together, we had nothing in common. This didn't happen often because we were different and it was hard especially for those getting in trouble.

Even in my orphanage home, some of the girls and boys were insensitive and impossible to get along with. They ended up being alone until they got used to living in our home. We used to say it came from their parents, maybe they were unkind because of how they were living. Most of them changed while growing up.

We went to school either in the morning or afternoon. When I was small we went in the mornings. After we were older, some went in the morning and some the afternoon. It depended on which grade we were in and what our job was during the year. We went for a half day and then we worked the second part of the day at our designated job. The ones going to school at eight in the morning went to their jobs after our lunch at twelve. Those who went to school in the afternoon at one, they went after the lunch hour. They would spend the morning working from eight to twelve. It worked out well for us and we learned how to do many things.

We even had a sewing department where some of the girls learned to make clothes. When we were getting ready to graduate, those sweet girls made our dresses for us. The senior girls got to pick out the material beforehand. Mine was blue with a white lace overlay. That dress was so pretty and I had a blue belt that was pleated to go around the waist. All the dresses were made alike, different in color with the white lace overlay.

At the time we didn't realize it, but they were preparing us to take care of ourselves once we graduated from high school and out on our own. Our jobs were given to us at the beginning of the year and then again during the summer months. Sometimes we would work two jobs during the year. It depended on our age primarily. I have no idea how they went about putting us in the different jobs. There were certain places I wanted to work. As a small child it didn't matter so much. When I was older I either wanted to work in the infirmary or the kitchen. Guess what, I got the opportunity to do both.

Younger girls worked in the dining rooms, waiting on tables. They set the tables and then cleaned up after the meals. We had dishwashers in each dining room so it made things easier for the girls to finish up after the meal. A teenager was the head girl in each of the dining rooms. They were responsible for the smaller girls working in the three different dining rooms.

I worked in the dining room for the older children. The dining room for the younger children was in the basement of the building. Upstairs were two dining rooms that held the middle age children and the older, high school children. We had a blessing we said three times a day. It goes like this:

> Father our God
> What we have here is of thee
> Accepts our thanks and blessings
> That we may continue to do thy will
> Amen

This is one blessing I don't say anymore because I say a different one each time I bless the food that is prepared for me. However, each year when we go home for our homecoming, we say this blessing and it brings a warmth to my body and I am so relaxed because I am home for the weekend and I don't know how many of my brothers and sisters are coming. I hope each year there is a stranger from the old days and then my eyes falls on their face, then my eyes travel to their eyes, and I know who it is. Our smiles give us away at times because of our love for one another.

My head girl in the large dining room was Mattie Lee Winfred. I loved this teenager so much, she took care of me and wouldn't let the boys at the tables tease or yell at me. I have seen her several times since leaving our orphanage home. She was one special big sister. The last time I saw her at homecoming she gave me her telephone number and we would talk back and forth for a few years.

Mattie Lee died a few weeks ago and Donald and I were at her graveside services. In my heart I had to be there to let her know how much I loved her. I saw her daughter again and also her niece at the service. They appreciated me being there. I told them how much I loved Mattie, they both had tears. After all, Mattie was my big orphan sister.

Thirteen

I WAS GROWING up and it was time for me to move on. This was when I went to the 2-G cottage, which means second girls' cottage. I was twelve when I arrived at the 2-G cottage. This was a nightmare for me because Pansy Burton was not my favorite counselor. As soon as I entered the 2-G my job became a cottage girl. Oh my, I thought at the time, should I go to see Ole Gray about this. I didn't want to be Mrs. Burton's cottage girl. This meant I cleaned the cottage every day and did whatever Mrs. Burton demanded of me and she was hard to get along with. Yet, she was a very attractive lady and I was told that she had been married but lost her husband in World War Two.

At that time I probably said, "Who would marry that witch?" Of course I wouldn't say that today, I know better. She really was a good person, but as a child I couldn't see the good in most of the cottage counselors.

I started my period while I was in this cottage. I had no idea what to do and how to do it. She handed me a Kotex and belt. "Here, Shelby, use it." I had to get another girl, who was already menstruating, to show me how to put the belt on with the Kotex.

We didn't get a whole box of Kotex, we only got one pad. We had to ask her for each pad during our cycle. It was embarrassing for the girls. She knew when we needed to change and when we were through with the cycle. This should have been a personal thing for us, but obviously it wasn't. I think she enjoyed seeing us embarrassed asking for pads. Some of the time when we knocked on her door she would get mad at us because she had to get up.

For a girl growing into a teenager it is important to have some personal time for herself. She knows her body is changing and so is her brain. We didn't get any personal time in my orphanage home. It was probably because there were so many of us. I do regret this because I was taught that it is ugly and gross to look at your body in certain places. Each time I wanted to look at myself, I remembered what Bobbie had threatened me with. I didn't want to get in trouble with Mrs. Burton.

I can still see Bobbie's face as she shouted out to me, "You are such a nasty girl, Shelby." It is still implanted in my subconscious. Of course, now I know better, but sometimes, while looking at my body, I can see Bobbie's face as she looked at me that awful day.

As a growing girl, looking at your body is normal. You want to see the breast and how much they have grown. Then you look at the waist to see if you actually have a good one. Your eyes travel slowly down your body to see how much has changed. I don't remember shaving my legs or underarms when I was growing up. I guess we did if we bought our own razor.

On the weekends we would sit around and talk during the afternoon, before the dinner bell rang the last time during the day. It was nice to be able to get to know other girls better. It gave us time to blend since each of us were different in looks and attitude, so if we wanted to be friends we needed time to blend together.

Mrs. Burton was also the one who noticed if we needed bras. She would send us to the ladies in the wardrobe section of the industrial building to tell her to fit us with a bra. Being the age of twelve to fourteen were hard years for me and some of the other girls. Our bodies were changing at a rapid rate and there was no one to talk to us about becoming a woman.

Three of my best friends came to my orphanage home during this time. Their names are Ernestine Harrison, Eoline Provost, and Jo Anne Mitchell. We had other friends during those years, but we are still good friends today and we stay in touch by phone and make it a point to see one another.

One Saturdays, while in the 2-G cottage, we sat around and talked—we didn't have television to keep us entertained.

Some went to the basement to talk or do their homework on the weekend.

Some of the boys and girls ran away at different times but most of the time they were brought back by Old Gray. Talking about running away and what we would do stayed with us for weeks. Finally, several of us decided to try it for the heck of it. I didn't like Pansy Burton so I thought if I got to Raleigh I could stay with my great aunt who taught school. Oh boy, what I planned was going to get me away from the witch of 2-G cottage.

There were maybe ten girls who were brave enough to consider running away for the heck of it. Why not, the boys were always running away. We talked about it for a few weeks and then that day came when we were going. It must have been close to Thanksgiving because we had vespers every night for a week. Ole Gray preached the sermon each night. I can't recall the date but I can say this, it was cold, I mean extremely cold. After we left the main building, those planning to leave the warmth of our beds stood together outside. As it turned out only three of us acknowledged our plans. The other seven girls reneged on us. Since I was one to take a dare, I wasn't going to renege. I was going to do what we planned even if it killed me. You could say that I was hardheaded and that remains today.

I can't for the life of me remember the third girl's name, maybe Mattie. But Eoline Provost and I were scared beyond recognition. We started walking. It was so dark and we had no idea where we were. We just kept walking . . . getting . . . tired . . . and . . . cold. The cold penetrated me to the point of wanting to start running to get warm. Of course, I couldn't do that, I was on the highway and I needed to see cars coming and going.

I thought to myself, "Why am I doing this, I'm so cold and my legs and feet are numb and tired."

Somehow we managed to walk quite far, all the way to the outskirts of Franklin, North Carolina. A car came by and the driver asked us if we needed a ride. We were scared because there were two young men in the car. Eoline and I said *no,* we were almost home.

Up ahead we could see lights in a house. We discussed it and didn't know if we should walk up to that house or not, not knowing who lived there. But we were afraid to keep walking because those boys could come back and see us still on the road.

So, we walked up to the door and knocked and a nice black woman let us in. She gave us some hot chocolate and wanted to know if we were hungry. We told her we were just tired and wanted to stay the night if she would let us. She didn't ask where we were from and we didn't offer the reason we were walking during the night and not home in bed, but I am sure she and her husband already knew.

Well, we all got in the bed together with our clothes on. We were so scared and cold, all we wanted was to get warm. The white sheets had been ironed and they felt so good to my poor freezing body. Sleep came fast because of the tiredness we felt.

The next morning, we made the bed up and left. We told the lady we were not hungry so we left probably around six since it was getting light enough to see. We thought she might ask where we were from and we would have to tell her the truth. Then she would have called the orphanage and Ole Gray would come for us.

We were so hungry and we could hear our stomachs rumbling. We saw a house down a long path. The house had to be warm with the smoke rising from the chimney. All I could think of was the warmth of the house, maybe some food in my stomach, and walking down the long path.

We walked down that long path petrified out of our minds. We didn't know what we would say once we knocked on the door. We would have to say that we were hungry so we could have something to eat before starting out again.

We knocked on the door. The woman let us in and cooked breakfast for us. She had to go into town and wanted to know if we wanted to ride with her. We had already told her the truth and we were going to Raleigh.

For some ungodly reason, she paid for us to take the bus to Raleigh. She had to go to an alteration shop to have a dress or coat hemmed, so we stayed with her for a few minutes and decided to go to the bus station and wait. Eoline and I noticed the women in the shop looking at us, obviously they knew where we were from. Naturally, we had not thought where the money would come from to go to Raleigh.

As we walked down the sidewalk, we saw a man coming toward us. As he got closer I could see that smile on his face. Ole Gray was a tall man and thin. He always dressed professionally. I don't think I ever saw him dressed casually.

I saw him first and said, "Oh, lordy, here comes Ole Gray. How in the world did he know we were in Franklin?"

He smiled and said, "You girls going somewhere?"

"We are going to Raleigh to stay with my aunt who teaches school there," I said.

Ole Gray smiled again and looked at me with concern. "Have you told your grandfather about leaving the orphanage?"

"No, I haven't thought about it."

"Don't you think he would like to know where you are going to be living?"

I didn't know what to say. We were caught leaving our home and going off without one cent of money. We didn't think about money at that time. Being twelve, we were never concerned about where our next meal would come from or where we were going to put our heads when we grew tired and needed sleep. In all, we had it made because we never needed money for anything on campus. Housing and food were always there for us.

He took us back to the orphanage and let us off at the infirmary. Mrs. Tomblin shook her head because she had to look after us for a week. She greased our head with Vaseline and that stuff that smelled to high heaven. She made us wear a rag around our head so the grease wouldn't soil our clothes or the bed.

How embarrassed we were because we had to go to school that way. When we got out of school each day we had to go back to the infirmary and wash windows. There were probably a hundred windows in that place—basement, first floor, and then the second floor.

I hated the basement of the infirmary. It was dark and spooky looking. Mrs. Tomblin made us wash those dirty windows in the part of the basement that were not used. She was letting us know that we should not be running away.

That part of the basement had not been used for years. At least it didn't look like it. I could hear whispering all around me as I washed those dirty windows. We three girls didn't talk at all during the time we were there. I could close my eyes and see soldiers from the civil war lying on the floor of that dark place. My mind was going so fast and all I wanted to do was to get out of there and go where normal people were. We did this for an entire week and boy was I one happy camper when Friday rolled around.

On Friday after school we went back to the 2-G cottage and Mrs. Burton. Oh boy, was I in trouble now. I had to face the witch of 2-G. I decided to look at her straight in the eyes and let her know how much I despised her. I wanted her to know how hateful she was to all of the girls.

She looked at each of us and wanted to know what our plans were. We shrugged and said nothing. I held my head high while she smiled and stared at me. She was letting me know I wasn't as smart as I thought I was. While she kept talking, I lifted my eyes and glared back at her. Oh boy, I was in a lot of trouble now. I chickened out and didn't open my mouth to say anything, only kept glaring at her until she finished yapping at us.

The next morning Mrs. Burton told me I would end up in the gutter after leaving my orphanage home. That woman said I would become a street person eating out of trash cans. She said I would sleep on the ground because I was a useless human being. Then she said I was a miserable specimen. In fact, she said . . . if . . . I . . . graduated. I never forgot those words she threw at me that day. Did she know how much she hurt me? Of course not and I felt that hurt for years. I told myself she would regret talking to me that way and after I became an adult.

After graduating, I started going back for our annual homecoming. When I saw Mrs. Burton I wouldn't speak to her. She tried to destroy me by putting me as low as she could. She might as well tell me she was rejecting me because I was a sorry-ass person. She made me determined to do better in every respect.

I thought I hated this woman. After I married Donald, I saw her one year at homecoming and I walked up to her. I told her what my husband did for a living and also what I did. I let her know that I had not ended up in the gutter. I outdid myself and told her I was doing great. I told her that I remembered the way she talked to me when I was twelve years old. She never apologized for saying those horrible things to me. In fact, I don't think she remembered saying those words.

That was the last time I spoke to her because the next year she retired and left the orphanage to finish out her life elsewhere. I never heard where she went to live. She treated the 2-G girls so bad and tried to put us in a category of the lowest of human lives. Everyone ended up going way above the gutter, and I'm not sure what some of the girls ended up doing but we didn't end up the way she wanted us to.

After growing up I didn't hate Mrs. Burton. She had her ways and maybe at that time she had a reason to be, as I would say, unpleasant to us.

I don't remember much more about the 2-G cottage. I was still a cottage girl for the rest of the year. I didn't get to change jobs the first of the year. I guess Ole Gray made me stay to teach me a very viable lesson. I gather Mrs. Burton didn't make it too hard for me since nothing else stands out in my older mind today.

Fourteen

IT'S STRANGE BECAUSE I don't remember much about the 3-G cottage. Nothing stands out so I guess I went about my life doing what I was told. I do remember Mrs. Johannsson was the cottage counselor, substituting for the regular counselor. She had the smallest feet for a body as round as hers.

This was the year I guess I really started becoming a young lady. By this time I was fifteen. I remember going to Mocksville, North Carolina. We were in the glee club and rode the bus a few hours for a competition there. I sat with my friend, Ovis Gibbs. She and I became good friends and we enjoyed doing things together. She graduated after me, I think two years later. Her brother, Charlie, was in my class and Oliver was a year ahead of me. Sammy, her youngest brother still had some time before graduating.

There was a fair at Mocksville so we got to have some fun before singing. It was so much fun riding the rides with Ovis that day. I remember the swings that made me sick as a dog when I got off. Ovis tried to get me to ride them again and I finally told her to forget it, I wasn't about to torture my body anymore.

It was late when we returned to our orphanage home. We had lunch in Mocksville but, for the life of me, I don't remember eating dinner. I'm sure we had bag dinners on the bus to eat. The bus happened to be one of the Greyhound Bus Lines that traveled around North Carolina. It was a huge bus and it held a lot of people. I don't remember if we went the second time or not, but probably did. In fact, I think we went several time to compete. Then again, I'm much older today and perhaps I don't remember a lot of things from back then.

THE HOLIDAYS AT the orphanage were great. When Easter came we didn't do anything special. On Saturday before Easter, Masons would come and have an Easter egg hunt for the small children. Only the small children were allowed to hunt for eggs. It was wonderful to hunt for the eggs and eat them until our stomachs hurt from all that sweet candy. I believe we had one for the girls and one for the boys. Of course if the boys and girls were together, the boys would probably find most of them or take them away from the girls.

During the summers, we worked at our jobs and tried to mind the supervisors. Well, at least some of us did as we were told. I was growing up fast and developing into a teenager. During the next couple of years I matured and enjoyed my life more.

I never had a boyfriend while in my orphanage home. I had several crushes, but they were not enough to go after a boy. I didn't want anything to do with them as far as being a girlfriend. I wanted them as friends and that was all. My mind was on other things like going to college to be a nurse and doing well throughout my life. I had planned to do well, regardless of what work I would do.

Then it was the fourth of July. We didn't do anything spectacular for this holiday. Since it was summertime we went swimming every day except Thursdays. That was the day the pool was emptied and cleaned. We just went on about our lives and enjoyed the summer months.

Everyone had to learn to swim. The big girls would get those who couldn't swim on the small diving board and tell them to put their hands over their head and then they would take a leg and send them directly into the pool. Even though it was hard at first, I learned to swim reasonably fast.

There were two or three big girls near the end of the small diving board to catch the ones learning to swim. They made sure the girls came to the top of the water. The big girls also held them while they tried to swim.

Then I was diving from the high diving board. I had a ball and the first time I got on the diving board I thought I was hot stuff. I loved swimming and still do today. Mozelle could dive from the high board and her legs and feet would be perfectly straight each time. I envied her because I couldn't quite do it.

The hours to swim were from one to four o'clock and we took turns going swimming for an hour each day. It depended on your age and the job you had during the summer months. It became a blessing to get away from work and spend one hour either swimming or laying out on the grass. The girls and boys swam separately.

Sometimes the boys would sneak out of the house and meet their girlfriends somewhere on campus. When the Chapel was built, I think most of them met in the basement. It was nothing to see one of the girls leaving during the night. For me there was no reason to have a boyfriend. I loved my life at that time doing what I relished, not being with some boy.

September was the month we got to go to the grape vineyard and eat all the grapes we could put in our stomachs. This was also my special time of the year when the weather was nice and the temperature was in the seventies. I love scuppernongs and I would eat until I got a stomachache, especially when I was young. They were the best thing that came our way during the month of September. Today, when they are in the grocery stores, I buy them and have a good time eating the whole container. They are one of my favorite things to eat. I love them almost as much as I love fried chicken and watermelons.

We had a watermelon feast each summer. It was in July or August. The large melons were sliced and everyone got a huge wedge to eat. Oh, it was so good and the coolness going down to my stomach made me a happy camper. I loved spiting those seeds out and trying not to drop any of my slice. Normally it was on a Saturday or Sunday afternoon. It could have been on the fourth of July. I remember it wasn't a school day.

Halloween as it is today was not observed while I was in my orphanage home. I never remember having a Halloween basket to receive candy from anyone. I do remember we had a Halloween carnival at school. Each class was responsible for certain things. I remember helping with the cakewalk in the eighth grade room.

One class had a bowl of pasta behind a dark curtain that was supposed to be brains. They kept the lights off in the room so those going in couldn't see anything. There was always bobbing for apples in one of the classrooms. It was a lot of fun for us and if we had some money we could buy a few things, like an apple.

We celebrated Thanksgiving Day with all the trimmings. Of course we were out of school for a few days, the way schools are today. The girls who worked in the dining rooms served the plates and oh, it was so good. We normally had some sort of desert but I don't remember what it was. I gather we went back to our cottages and played as a youngster or talked to others when we were older. In the 4-G cottage we probably watched television during the afternoon. I do remember singing Thanksgiving songs during the season especially at church. From the time I was fourteen, I was either working in the kitchen or hospital. I would have my Thanksgiving meal there.

Some of us would pick up our library book and read. Mrs. Tomblin taught me how important it was to read, whether it be fiction or nonfiction. It could have been a historical book, because I learned a lot about our country. I loved books about nurses and I read every one of these in the library.

If I remember correctly, we had a bag supper on Thanksgiving. The bag supper consisted of peanut butter and molasses sandwich and a piece of fruit. We didn't go to the dining room for the bag supper. It was delivered to the cottages and we ate there. This was one time I don't care that stupid bell rang the dinner hour.

During the year, Masons were always coming to visit the orphanage. Jo Ann and I were lucky because we got to show them around the campus. There was one couple that enjoyed being with Jo and me. They were the Bowers from Southern Pines, North Carolina. They came every year and when we graduated we both got a nice piece of luggage to use.

I sent them a wedding notice when Donald and I got married. They sent me a beautiful lace tablecloth which I still have. We went to Southern Pines to visit with them several times with our children. They never had children and I think Jo and I became their children in a roundabout way. We visited several times before Mr. Bowers died. He was with the Postal Service. I really loved this couple a lot. Even Lynn got a gift from them at Christmas.

It was always nice when Masons came to visit. I always wanted to show them around the campus and how we lived. Sometimes they were there at mealtime and they ate in the teacher's dining room. Most of them gave us some money for taking our time to show them around.

Fifteen

CHRISTMAS WAS A special time for all the orphans. The cottage girls trimmed the tree with balls, lights, and angel hair and they were so pretty. I loved the lights on the tree when they were turned on at nighttime and we could see how beautiful it was. On Christmas morning we got to open our gifts that were under the tree. I got a few gifts from the Masons. I don't remember getting one gift from my family. Jo Ann also said we never got a gift from any member of our family during the Christmas season.

The Masons also gave us a box of Life Savers and we got a stocking with nuts, candy, and raisins in it. I loved the raisins because they were dried on the stem. The box of candy we got wasn't my favorite at all. I would exchange the candy for raisins. To this day I love raisins. We normally got a few gifts from a certain Mason. We would open them up and be completely surprised.

I don't remember getting anything from Santa Claus. It didn't happen in my orphanage home, maybe the baby cottage but that was all. We stayed in the cottages after our Christmas feast at lunch. We had a bag supper on Christmas Night, again made of peanut butter and molasses sandwiches and fruit.

As I remember we got out of school for a week or two the same as schools do today. It was nice, but we still had our jobs to do whether school was out or not. We never slept late, always up at six a.m. Christmas time was always enjoyable and we loved each and every item we got during the season.

SUNDAY MORNINGS WE walked downtown to church. This was the law for us as long as we lived in the orphanage. We always walked to church and it wasn't bad at all. We got to spend time with our friends as we took that long walk to town each Sunday. There was a sidewalk from the campus to downtown so we didn't have to walk on the road because it would have been dangerous especially on Sunday mornings with so many of us.

On Sunday night we had vespers and Ole Gray preached so we stayed on campus. Jo and I went to the Presbyterian Church because that was the church we went to before going to our orphanage home. There were not as many going to the Presbyterian Church. Most went to the Baptist or Methodist Churches.

I was baptized when I was thirteen. There were a few of us orphans who received the honor at the Presbyterian Church in Oxford. I thought I was grown when I was baptized.

I loved going to this church every Sunday and loved the pews arranged in a semi-circle. It was not the biggest church in Oxford, not by a long shot. However, it was one of the prettiest churches I've ever seen.

I would love to be able to walk in the Presbyterian Church again to bring back those good memories I have stored in my heart. I can close my eyes and still see what this church looks like on the inside. One day when I am at homecoming I'm going to see if the door is open so I can go in and sit in the section I did as a child and then a teenager. In fact, I plan to do it this year in October.

Since I mentioned walking to church, I must go ahead and tell you about the Episcopal Church and the rumor that went around for the little ones walking to church. We walked in a line of two with a supervisor going with us each Sunday. I don't even remember who the supervisor was and I don't remember if any orphan went to the Episcopal Church. I think we went in the rain, cold, or heat. Maybe not in the snow but I am sure we went in the rain if it wasn't coming down too hard.

There were not many Sundays we didn't walk to church. Going to church was instilled in us by the time we entered our orphanage home. All orphans grow up knowing about God and going to church. This was an important part of who we were when we left after graduating from high school.

There are several boys who became ministers after leaving our home. A few of them are Bobby Garner, Bill Everett, Tommy Jones, and Ray Brickhouse. I knew Bobby, Bill, and Tommy because they were closer to my age. Ray is still a young man and I met him one year when we were getting out of our car that first day of homecoming. We were parked on the main road close to the administration building. He has preached two times, that I know of, at homecoming and I'm hoping he will be giving us the message again this year. After talking to this young man I see how much he loves his Lord. He and his family are such nice people and of course he is my orphan brother.

Anyway, the Episcopal Church was on the corner of two streets, one of them being College Street and the graveyard was directly behind the church. I don't remember the name of the other street. There wasn't a large parcel of land for graves, so I think maybe they were the old ones from many years ago. Anyway, there was this great legend going around the campus about the graveyard being creepy.

I didn't believe in those things but, for some foolish reason, I listened to orphans talk about it. I remember people telling me that as you walk by the Episcopal Church you should never point your index finger toward that old graveyard.

The reason was, "If you point your index finger toward the graveyard your finger will rot off." I don't think I believed it, but I didn't point my index finger. In fact I probably wouldn't do it today.

I never pointed in the direction of the graveyard as long as I was in my orphanage home, not even as a teenager. I'm talking about holding my arms down by my sides so my arm wouldn't be out just in case my index finger would point toward that graveyard by mistake. I never pointed any of my fingers toward that graveyard. I'm not superstitious but I don't want to chance it. Yeah, yeah, I'm a big Winnie, so what.

Since I'm older now and it's not that I'm afraid, but it's instilled in me not to point. Nowadays that's my excuse. I say, "Pointing is not good manners. See how easy it is? I don't have to say anymore. What would your excuse be if you walked by that church today? Do you think your finger would rot off? If you try it, don't blame me for telling you about this legend?"

I AM GROWING older in the 3-G so I think I am a big-shot. I can't remember who slept next to me. It was a dormitory setting like the other cottages. The only cottage that had different rooms was the 4-G. We couldn't wait to get to this cottage. It meant we were getting ready to graduate in the next two or three years. This was the first cottage on the right when we turn on the main road.

Being an orphan didn't bother me. I knew what an orphanage was and I knew why I was there. Papa didn't come to see us much during the ten years we were there, maybe two times all together. It didn't matter to either Jo or me, we already had our orphanage family and they were the ones that counted for us.

I was hurt at times when some of the orphans' parents would come. Tommy Jones' sister would come back to see him and also his mother. John Belk's mother came often and I remember seeing her. She was a beautiful lady as I recall. My aunt and uncle probably came two times during our ten years we were growing up in the orphanage. My dad's family never came that I can remember, but our dad came a few times and he was always drunk, having to sleep it off at the infirmary. It was so embarrassing for us to see him this way.

There were some orphans who never had visitors. They didn't seem to mind as far as I recollect. We were happy orphans just being together. I never got into a fight with another orphan because of the love I had for them. I didn't see the need to hit anyone when we got plenty of those from our cottage counselors or teachers.

Sixteen

HEE-HAW, I am now in the 4-G cottage. I was a big girl and, by George, I knew it. In this cottage we had separate rooms for the girls. Jo Ann was able to come to the 4-G cottage, too. It was nice having my sister with me. We still didn't room together and I have never understood the reason. At that time I really thought we could room together. Oh well, that's par for the course with us growing up in our orphanage home. I roomed with three other girls and we even had closets to hang up our good clothes. Two of my roommates were Betty Jean Moore and Eoline Provost. I can't remember who the third girl was. I want to say it was Janice but it wasn't because I was rooming with her sister, Betty Jean. I had the bed at the window and I loved the cool breeze that came through during the summer months.

Mrs. Woodruff was the counselor. We called her *Bear Woodruff* because she was a big lady, I mean really big. When it was time for lights out at night, she would come to the foot of the stairs and yell, "This is the Bear, cut those lights out and get to sleep."

I can't remember ever seeing her upstairs. She weighed a lot and I'm sure she couldn't make it up those steps to the second floor. Lights went out at ten each and every night in the big girls' cottage. She was strict, but she was such a softy, a lamb in my book, and I liked her, regardless. She was my favorite counselor by far.

When she tried to be a tough lady we all knew she wouldn't do anything. I've seen her correct someone and then turn from them and smile. I loved watching her do this in the basement when we were doing our homework.

I was good at hurrying to finish my homework so I could read the book I got from the library. I'm sure she thought I never studied since she was always asking me if I was through with my homework. She would see me reading a library book and I'm sure she thought I was being lazy. Working in the kitchen or the teachers' dining room, I had time to do some of my homework while at my job. I always told her the truth and said yes I had finished when she called out to me.

My friend Ovis had a cousin in the air force and I started writing to him. Now I was really a big shot. I always wrote him back when I received a letter from him. He sent me a beautiful blue necklace and earrings for Christmas my last year there. It was so pretty, but too dressy to wear just anytime. I saved it to wear for something special. I had that necklace until this year when I decided to clean out my jewelry box. I still have a part of the necklace I decided to keep. I even wear that necklace now and then when I need something blue to wear.

He was older and wanted to come to see me after I graduated. I was living with my aunt and uncle at the time. They thought it best for me not to see him since I didn't know him. They were trying to protect me, so I didn't question them because they were looking after me during this time. This is one time I guess I can say thank you to them.

We would get so bored during the summer. These are the times we would decide to do something sneaky. I would set my alarm clock to twelve and when it rang I hurriedly cut it off so no one could hear it. I kept it under the covers so the Bear couldn't hear it. I jumped up and woke the other girls and we would sneak downstairs, get our bathing suits from outside, and put them on in the furnace room. The furnace room was where the coal was kept to put in the furnace to help warm the building during the winter months.

As we ran to the pool, we stopped ever so often to hide behind one of the large oak trees. Then we would run again. I don't remember all who went but I think Janice, Betty Jean, Ovis, Eoline, and me. Maybe Ernestine Harrison and Jo Anne Mitchell went also. The same girls went every time and others didn't know about it, or we didn't invite them to come with us.

Swimming in the wee hours of the morning was fantastic. It made our day because it was a no-no. It was so refreshing since there was no air conditioning in the cottages. So going swimming in the middle of the night was wonderful for us and we did this the entire summer. However, Bear Woodruff might have known, but she never let on to any of us. I am estimating she just let it slip her mind unless we were seen by someone else on campus and reported us to her.

I remember one of my friends was responsible for keeping the furnace going during the winter months. Her name was Frances Hildebrand. She would make costumes from toilet paper or tissue paper and dance around the basement on Saturday and Sunday. There was always a flower made of toilet tissue for her hair. She wanted to be a movie star so bad. Today I don't know where she ended up or even if she is still living. As I recalled, she was one of those neat girl you never forget. I think someone told me that she had died years ago.

Janice Moore and I babysat Ole Gray and Mrs. Gray's dog when they went out of town. I used to spend more time than necessary at their house. I would look in the refrigerator to see what I could eat. Since it wouldn't be food from the orphanage kitchen, I thought it would be better. The one thing they never had was chewing gum and candy. I'm guessing they didn't care for it, so I was left empty handed. The one thing I wanted, they didn't have, and I mean every time they were gone.

I always had to look after that stupid dog of Mrs. Gray. Ole Gray paid me some money for doing this job even though I enjoyed it because I would stay at their house for long periods of time and watch television.

Janice and I looked after that stupid dog for over a year. She would bark like crazy at the least sound. She didn't want to go outside to get busy, nor did she want to be walked. She was a tiny dog and she barked when we walked into the house. I absolutely hated that barking Chihuahua dog.

Living in the 4-G cottage was by far the best place for me. I used to go downtown for Bear Woodruff to get her candy or ice cream. If I got her ice cream I had to hurry back so it wouldn't melt. She didn't have a car so she depended on the girls to buy things for her. Evidently, I was one of her favorites because she would give me money to buy something for me, too.

Bear Woodruff was an okay lady in my book. She was not as bad as some of the girls said she was. If you stayed on her good side, she treated you with respect. This large lady was a lamb, but could be mean if you stepped out of your boundaries. We had to heed what she said and know if she was feeling okay before asking for something.

I remember I brought a hot dog home from the kitchen for Shirley Alford once. She was playing basketball late that night and didn't eat much at dinner. Her game was the last game of the evening and she normally ate very little before playing because it upset her stomach. I was working in the kitchen so it was easy for me to sneak the hot dog with all the good stuff on it for her. The only thing was the smell of onions piled high on that dog.

Ms. Johannsson was filling in for the Bear for some reason. Evidently, Bear Woodruff was on vacation or someone in her family was sick. By the way, Bear Woodruff had two daughters who were in our orphanage home and they called her Bear, too. They were treated just like the rest of us and if they did something wrong, they were in trouble with her, too.

Anyway, this woman didn't even wake me before she slapped me hard across the face. The next morning I was going downstairs to leave for school and she started in on me again. I said to her, "You better not ever slap me again when I'm asleep if you know what is best."

She yelled and told me, "Hold out your hands so I can hit you with the ruler I'm holding." There was no way I was going to let her hit me again.

I touched the last step coming from the upstairs. I turned and said, "I am going to Ole Gray's and report you. You have no business hitting anyone while they are sleeping." That is exactly what I did and he hugged me and told me not to worry, he would handle it.

WHEN ONE OF the kitchen girls had a birthday, we would have a party and got to invite boys each time. Mrs. Harris would chaperon us on that night since she was in charge of the kitchen girls. Of course we weren't out late. We had to be in bed by ten every night so I would say the party was over by nine, giving us time to get to our cottage and get ready for bed.

Those days were very special for all of us hardworking kitchen girls. We always played spinning the bottle. We had to kiss the boy the bottle pointed to. It was creepy for those who had never kissed a boy before and it made us a little timid. If the bottle neck pointed to a boy or girl we didn't care for, it was too bad, we had to kiss them, regardless. It was a lot of fun during those precious years of growing up in our orphanage home. Those memories are so precious to me and I love sitting here remembering some of the boys I kissed when we went into another room and the lights were out. We didn't kiss the boy in front of any one, we did that behind closed doors.

The girls working for Mrs. Harris were treated well. She liked us a lot, especially those of us who loved working with her. Living in town, she also had a family. I remember her having grandchildren and I thought that was the neatest thing. Most of the kitchen girls loved this lady and especially me. I thought she was the greatest thing ever.

Seventeen

AFTER THE CHAPEL was built, we had dances in the basement. The football and baseball coaches planned a banquet for the players every year and it was held in the basement. Even the meal was served in the basement. It was fun to be asked to go with one of the players.

When I was a junior I went with Dickie Powell. At that time I had burned my arm in the egg steamer. I opened the door and stuck my arm in too fast to get the eggs out. I was always in a hurry, not waiting not one second before I stuck my arm in that steamer. The steam was terribly hot and it burned rather quickly. I could be such a dodo at times when I was younger. I am still that way sometimes.

I had to go to see Mrs. Tomblin at the infirmary. She bandaged my arm up with Vaseline and that stuff that smelled so bad. I didn't want go and smell terrible. However, the day of the banquet I asked if I could just use Vaseline. She smiled and said yes. As it turned out, I was allergic to that awful smelly, greasy stuff. Had a good time and enjoyed some good food that was cooked in our kitchen. I also had a great time dancing with the boys. We knew most of the dances that were popular during that time and we used up that extra energy we had stored in our bodies. I don't remember anyone sitting on the sidelines and not dancing at events.

The next day, on Saturday morning, I had to go back to have my arm checked by Mrs. Tomblin and it was almost healed. She was pleased she had not put the awful smelly stuff on my arm. The Vaseline did the trick and off the bandage came for good. I remember how she smiled at me and gave me a loving pat on my butt as I turned to go out of the room.

When I was a senior I went to the football banquet with Charlie Gibbs. It was a nice outlet on a Friday night and it was fun to dance. I enjoyed dancing then and still do today.

I REMEMBER PLAYING basketball. We didn't play other schools, we had different teams that were put together, called intramural teams. I was always a guard but I wanted to be a forward so bad. Gabe Austell wouldn't let me. He always told me I was a good guard so I had to stay a guard every year. During those years, players could not go across the middle line. You had to stay on your side of the court or you fouled.

I remember so many time Gabe yelling at me, "Shelby, you're fouling." I don't remember if we got five fouls for you to foul out of the game. I remember playing and it thrilled me to take the ball from one of my friends. The boys were allowed to watch the game if they wanted to.

I loved playing all sports. I was on the team that won the girls' speed ball championship. It is similar to soccer. The girls had softball teams, also. We loved being outside where we could play different sports. Miss Pender was the coach and all the girls seem to love her. I didn't because I remembered what she did to Carolyn Caldwell years before, trying to force her to swim. I tolerated her and did what she told me, but that was all because I couldn't forgive her for bullying my friend in such a horrible way.

Miss Pender left the orphanage when I was in the eleventh grade. When she left, she took Sally Groome, an orphan in our orphanage home, with her. Sally cleaned Ms. Pender's room and normally she was there all Saturday afternoon. All the orphans and counselors were shocked at the accusation of kidnapping because it had never happened before.

Reports were on the news, television, and radio all the way to the state of New York and as far west as Arizona. It was a big thing because it was a kidnapping. I don't know what happened when they were found, but I have heard that Sally lived with Miss Pender and went to college.

We never heard anything from them again. I don't know if Miss Pender was prosecuted or not. The orphans were never told the outcome. I don't think she was prosecuted because I think we would have heard about it. I am almost certain Miss Pender was gay and that is the reason she kidnapped Sally.

OUR FOOTBALL TEAM was always great. With Gabe Austell as head coach and Garland Talton as assistant coach how could they not be good? Our team was made up of boys who could hit hard and be hit just as hard. There were no crybabies on the team from Oxford Orphanage.

We were able to go to the games that were played at home. We hated that we couldn't see Oxford Orphanage Red Devils play at Webb High School. Webb and our team, the Red Devils were big rivals because Webb High Warriors were from the town of Oxford. The boys from Webb used to come on campus before a game, and it turned into a shouting match on the main road. They hated us and we couldn't stand them. There was never a fight. At least, I don't think there was. It was more or less just a shouting match. Of course, the orphans would win the shouting match every time.

The only time we were allowed to go out of town to see our team play was when we went to Raleigh to play different teams at the North Carolina State University Football Stadium. I don't remember why we were allowed to go to this game except it was held by the Shriners of North Carolina and it was called The Shrine Bowl Game.

It was so much fun going out of town for this game. It was one of the most important times for us orphans. Especially if we were playing The Methodist Home for Children in Raleigh. Of course, The Methodist Home for Children was one of our big rivals, too.

MOST OF THE high school orphans were members of the glee club. We always went to Meredith College in Raleigh for competition. It was fun to be away from home for a few hours. We normally came away with good scores and even won a few times.

We rode the Greyhound bus and that was a big treat for all of us. The orphanage didn't have a bus to take us so we always used Greyhound buses. I can't recall who we sang against but we gave it our all every time. We enjoyed the glee club and Miss Peacock was a great music teacher. She was extremely good and stayed on our butts until we had the songs down pat. She even wrote our Alma Mater that we sing at homecoming on Sunday morning.

At homecoming each year we go to the chapel at ten o'clock on Sunday morning for a good sermon and singing hymns. For two years, Ray Brickhouse has given us a good one. Ray is married and has children of his own. After the sermon we sing our Alma Mata. It always brings a chill to me because I do love singing it.

Eighteen

WE WERE ALLOWED two weeks of vacation each summer if we had been good throughout the year. Jo and I always went to Papa's. Those two weeks away from our orphanage home were great because we worked and got paid. Jo and I worked in tobacco to earn money for our school clothes and we didn't have to share these when we were in the 4-G. It was a nasty job but at least we made money doing it. We were used to doing nasty jobs so it didn't matter. She and I would have done anything to make the money to buy our own clothes. Those years were when we were between thirteen and seventeen.

When we were in the 3-G and 4-G cottage we could buy our own clothes if we had the money. We could have more than the allotted amount issued to each person every year. I loved buying my own clothes because it made me feel good. I used the money wisely though because I wore some of those clothes to a job after I graduated.

My first year at the orphanage, Jo and I went home for two weeks at Christmas but that was the last year we were away during the Christmas season. Papa gave us each a stretchable bracelet and it was one of two gifts we got from him during the ten years we were living in our orphanage home. Even afterwards he never gave us anything at all, not even a penny.

Becoming an adult started when I went to the 4-G cottage to live for two years. It was time to think about what I wanted to do once I left. There were times I wanted to be a nurse. Then there were times I wanted to design women's clothing. I knew I wanted to excel, regardless of the profession.

Most of the orphans had dreams of a good profession if they studied hard and made good grades. Of course, none of us thought about getting married right away except those who were going steady and knew they were going to get married. Only a few of those I can still recall.

Betty Evans and Robert Wyatt were one couple that got married shortly after leaving our orphanage home. Another couple was Jack Barger and Mary Ann Adcock. Also in this group were Leroy Dixon and Betty Jean Truitt.

One summer while we were on vacation, my mother's brother came to see Papa and asked Jo Ann and I if we wanted to go home with him for a few days. He lived in Florence, South Carolina and it was a long ways from Willow Springs, North Carolina. Jo didn't want to go anywhere, but I wanted to go so I could be with his daughter, Jean, and have fun. I was thirteen or fourteen at the time.

At that time he ran an outdoor movie theater. He took me shopping for clothes to wear while I was there. We shopped at Belk's in Fuquay before we left to travel to Florence. This was unusual for any member of my family, but he let me pick out what I wanted. I enjoyed those few days so much.

I met a boy who worked for him at the drive-in theater. This guy was really neat and we had a good time the entire time I was there. Jo really missed out on this trip. I could have cared for the boy, but being in the orphanage, it wouldn't have been wise to continue a courtship with him. Kissing was fun during the few days we spent together. Today I have no idea what that good-looking boy's name was or how he looks now.

IT WAS ALWAYS nice to be home and not have to do things at a certain time each day. I was able to sleep in if we were not barning tobacco. The tobacco stained our hands but we could wash it off when we got back to the house each day. The gum was easy to remove but the stains were still there for a week.

During my two weeks of vacation on Papa's farm, I handed tobacco to the person who was looping it. When each stick was full, it was laid on the ground and another one was started. This went on for the entire day except when we stopped for an hour at lunchtime. My aunt always left the barn early to cook for the family and some of the other workers. Most of workers ate with the family.

We always had fresh corn, beans, tomatoes, and cucumbers to eat for lunch. There were days when we got fresh string beans which became one of my favorites. Then she would cook up some pork chops or fry some chicken. If we were lucky we might get some fried corn bread.

I was used to fried chicken because we had it for Sunday lunch at our orphanage home every week. My aunt could fry up some good corn bread with the fried chicken which I still love today. She gave me a recipe for her fried corn bread and I still make it. Of course, it is fried and not good for our bodies but boy, it was something special at those lunches with all those fresh vegetables coming from the garden.

The day was started early when we barned tobacco. The men and boys were out in the field at sunrise each morning. It didn't take long to get a full slide of tobacco for the women and girls to string onto sticks.

When there were no more slides of tobacco to come from the fields, the men and boys came to the barn where the girls and women were working. Then the tobacco had to be put in the barn to cure.

The barns had a high-pitched roof and sectioned off evenly so the sticks could be handed up and placed on these sections to cure out. The women and girls had to hand the sticks of tobacco up to the men and boys who put them in place.

Talk about hard; this was the hardest part. Those sticks of green tobacco were very heavy while I was holding them up, waiting for a boy or man to grab them from me. The sticks were placed exactly the right way so they would cure evenly. The men were tired and so were the women at the end of the day.

Working in tobacco was hard but it paid well for this orphan. Most of the time the day finished up around five o'clock. I had stood the entire day except maybe an hour we took for lunch.

After the barn was full of tobacco my uncle would stay at the barn all night to keep the wood burning at a certain temperature to cure the tobacco. He would sleep on the table where the tobacco was laid out for handing when the slides came in. The next day he worked hard again and didn't seem to be tired after not getting much sleep. He would again stay at the barn all night. Being a farmer back then was tiresome and if there was little or too much rain it could destroy the crops that had taken so much time to plant.

I don't remember how much money I made but it satisfied Jo and me. We sure didn't have much money at the orphanage, but we did get an allowance when we were older. It was less than five dollars a month, so it wasn't much at all. I only used that allowance for going to the movies if we were allowed. I always had popcorn and a drink.

Aunt Janie or her daughter always took Jo and me to Raleigh to buy our shoes and school clothes before we were due back at the orphanage. It was great to go back to our orphanage home with lots of new stuff to wear. I loved the latest designs and if they were not too expensive I would buy something that was the hottest thing from Hudson Belk. I even thought I was hot stuff when I went back home after being away for two weeks each summer.

I loved going shopping and still do today. I still go to Belk's to buy most of my clothes to buy the latest styles.

We didn't get any soft drinks in the orphanage. We had milk or water to drink. We never had tea for mealtime like people do today. Of course, coffee wasn't heard of unless you worked in the kitchen or teacher's dining room. Snacks were not heard of in the orphanage. I think the one good thing we had was our ice cream,- which all of us loved.

I felt like a queen each summer after I had worked hard helping my family barn their tobacco. Normally we stayed with Papa during the two weeks each summer. He was routinely overseeing all his farms and we didn't get to spend much time with him.

His two stepdaughters and great granddaughter were always there so we bunked in with my unmarried aunt in her room. There was never anywhere for Jo and me to stay as long as they were there.

It seemed so unfair that he put Jo and me in the orphanage and let his wife's daughters and granddaughter live with them. He kept them up and furnished clothing for them. His step-granddaughter was my age and he made sure she had nice clothes to wear. The two daughters never worked on the farm. I guess they thought they were too good to be doing dirty work like that. They had it made when their mother married Papa.

He never offered to give us money to take home with us. We were probably a burden during the two weeks we were there. I do remember one time when I was helping to barn tobacco and I got sick. The dew in the morning was normally high and of course, I walked barefooted just about everywhere at the orphanage and on the farm.

My leg was swollen and I got deathly sick from it. Papa took me to the doctor, and I had blood poisoning that came from a mosquito bite on my foot. Walking through the dew and then getting tobacco stains on the area, my leg was huge and I had a red streak running up my leg.

This was one time I stayed home for several days with my foot elevated with pillows. I had to lay on Papa's bed because it was close to the kitchen and my step-grandmother didn't have far to walk far to tend to me. She showed a slight caring for me during this time.

She never told me she loved me because she didn't know me. Even after we graduated from our orphanage home she never seem to care for Jo or me. When we went to see Papa she always cooked a great meal, but that was all. Hey, she never exerted any energy on us. She cooked lunch every day, regardless. She just made a little more.

WHEN WE WENT back to the orphanage we were happy to be with our orphan brothers and sisters again. We missed our routine when we were not there. Our routine schedule was so messed up when we were gone and even the meals were messed up. It was hard to get back on track.

During the two weeks we had fun with the cousins, but when they went to a movie, we had to stay home most of the time because we didn't have any money. Papa never offered us the money for a movie. Once in a while my aunt would give us the money. The money from working in tobacco was used for clothing.

Before we went to our orphanage home, Papa also grew cotton. When it was time to harvest the cotton, we kids had to help pick it. We had a long sack that we put over our head and let hang under our arms to put the cotton in. We would fill that bag several times during the day. Then we took it to the house where someone weighed the cotton.

All this was done in the fall. Evidently, we stayed home from school to help house the cotton. I was in the second and third grades. Too young to be in the fields but we, along with my cousins, worked during that time, regardless..

Jo Ann and I learned, at an early age, to have chores to do. We certainly didn't complain because we were used to it. In fact, I still stay on a schedule most of the time. It was instilled in me when I was growing up in my orphanage home.

During the late fall we would grade the tobacco we had cured during the summer months. It was really nasty, to say the least. The tobacco was a golden color and it would make a mess with small pieces in the air, making it hard to breathe. This was done in what we called the tobacco house. It was warm and toasty in the room during the cold days.

Nineteen

THERE WAS AN outside skating rink between the baby cottage and the kitchen in the orphanage. We were free on the weekend to go skating. Most of the smaller children were the ones to skate. The big girls and boys didn't use it much. Most of the children had skates and we had fun skating around the rink. I loved to skate real fast and then turn around. Some of the time I would fall trying to show off. I remember I fell more than once and skinned my knees.

One time I had my skate key in my hand and when I fell I landed on my hand holding the key. It caused a bad cut on the palm of my hand. I got a few stitches from Mrs. Tomblin and I believe the stitches hurt worse than the key. I was probably ten at the time. As we got older we forgot about the skating rink.

Close by was a jungle gym we could climb on. This was fun, but we girls had to be careful since we didn't wear shorts or long pants. It was also near the kitchen and the dining rooms. Since it was close to the baby cottage, they could play every day if it was nice outside.

One time I had climbed to the top of the jungle gym and when I started back down I lost my footing and fell to the ground. Man, the hurt was so bad I couldn't walk. Some of the girls got a wagon from the Baby Cottage and put me in it and pulled me to the infirmary. By the time Mrs. Tomblin saw me I was able to stand again. Of course, I was sore as heck and I was that way for about a week. I think this is where I began having back problems.

I don't recollect getting hurt again as long as I was in the orphanage. We had P.E. two or three times a week in high school. As hard as we girls played, we never got hurt because we were tough. We never fought so we didn't get hurt throwing punches. We were tough due to working every day somewhere in our orphanage home and not complaining. Yeah, we were so tough, and even today most of us still have that toughness in us.

Of course we, or I should say my friends and I, never fought over anything. In fact, I don't remember fussing with anyone during the ten years I was in the home. I was a happy person just about the entire time I was there.

Thinking back, I never saw anyone having a fist fight. Maybe the boys fought but we girls didn't. We solved our problems either by talking it out or just forgetting what made us mad in the first place. I'm sure the boys fought, but it was done at their cottages or outside, behind their cottage.

I am now an older teenager and my time in my orphanage home was precious to me. There were so many of us that were friends and we always found something to occupy our time. We got our first televisions when I was in the 4-G cottage and we got to see the different shows coming on at night. Oh boy, that was so much fun. I remember seeing comedies and we would laugh at seeing people act silly.

On Saturday afternoons we would gather in the basement to watch television. Ivy Lee Radford tried her best to get all of us to fight her about the television. She would get in front of the screen so the rest of us couldn't see. We would yell at her and she wouldn't move.

We would go over and pull her back but, guess what, she moved even closer. The only person who could get her to move was my friend, Janice. I don't know what magic Janice used but Ivy Lee would only move for her. She was the most determined girl I have ever known, determined to have her way at any cost. I never saw her again after she graduated.

We were able to walk downtown to the movies when we were teenagers if we had money. I enjoyed going downtown and buying popcorn and a drink. That was a great big deal to all of us. We normally would go on Saturday afternoon and be back home by dinner time. Seeing the Lone Ranger was one of my favorites and I loved the western movies. Still do.

I enjoyed Zorro movies because they were fast moving and I liked the actor especially. He was so good looking. I have no idea what his name was but I sure did like looking at him.

There were others I enjoyed seeing, but Doris Day was by far my favorite actress. Then there was Cary Grant that I enjoyed along with Mary Martin and James Stewart. Those days were wonderful because we got to see the latest styles of clothing and shoes. I have always been told I look like Mary Martin and Mitzi Gaynor. I don't see it, but if others thought so, it was okay with me. My favorite singer was Mario Lanza. He had the most beautiful voice. Of course he sang opera and my friends thought I was crazy to like him.

Since we were free on Saturday afternoon, I started cleaning some of the teacher's rooms. Just about all the teachers lived on campus. They lived above the administration offices which were on the first floor. They only had a bedroom they stayed in. I do not recollect if any of the teachers had cars.

I cleaned Miss Shield's room every Saturday. Then there was Miss Baldwin's room that I cleaned every other week. Miss Shield was the seventh grade teacher and Miss Baldwin taught the fifth grade. Miss Baldwin failed me my first year in the fifth grade. I use to tell people I failed so Jo Ann and I could be together, but I don't really know if that is the reason. I probably wasn't doing my homework in the fifth grade. I did enjoy being in the class with my sister though.

I became friendly with both of these teachers when I was cleaning their rooms. There were a few more that I cleaned, but my memory doesn't recall who they were. One of the teachers I think was Miss Simpson. Miss Shields and Miss Baldwin always gave me more than what I charged them. They set the amount of money for having their rooms cleaned but whatever the amount was it was okay with the girls doing the cleaning.

They were very appreciative of me cleaning their rooms each week on Saturday afternoons. They would give me some of their hand-me-down jewelry. I liked the jewelry and I wore it to school or church each week. Most of the jewelry were necklaces and even if I didn't care for the ones they gave me, I took them, regardless. Then I would give it to one of my friends.

Downstairs where the administration had their offices was a candy section. We called it the candy corner. My best friend, Janice Moore, was the administration girl Friday for at least two years. She didn't change jobs the way the rest of us did. It used to make me so envious of her because of the candy.

She didn't have to pay as much for hers as the rest of us did. I loved going to see her to buy penny candy such as sugar daddies, bit-of-honeys, and Mary Janes. Beechnut and Bazooka bubble gum were my favorite gum. I loved that gum and if I could find it today, I would buy enough to last a long time. I don't chew gum anymore, but if I had Beechnut I would start again. Best gum anywhere.

Twenty

WHEN I WORKED in the kitchen, I would listen to the radio on Sunday mornings. I loved listening to the big bands. Stan Kenton and Bennie Goodman were my favorite. I enjoyed classical and jazz, so I listened to Artie Shaw and other jazz musicians. The other girls didn't like me listening to classical because of the opera singers.

They thought I was a little off listening to "crap" as they called it. I don't know whose radio it was, but I think it was mine. We didn't listen to the radio in the 4-G cottage. It had to be mine because I took a radio home with me when I graduated from high school.

The girls, who worked in the kitchen, had to work every other Sunday to cook lunch. Mrs. Harris always let us listen to the music on Sunday morning because there wasn't much noise from others coming through for some reason. The girls who were in the eleventh grade worked the morning shift and went to school in the afternoon. The senior girls worked the afternoon shift. We went to school in the mornings and came in to work at lunch time.

So on the weekends we got a few hours off to stay at the cottage and do our thing. I remember that I read a lot of books during this time. I found out that I loved cooking. I still love trying new recipes and using different spices for flavor. I even help cook for my church today.

Mrs. Dora Harris was a great teacher. She was special in every way and she taught me how to fry chicken so it would be crispy and so good. I never heard her complain when we asked her how to make something. She was a wonderful person and a great friend. She and Mr. Pruitt worked well together making up the menus for a week. It was posted where the kitchen girls could see what they would have to cook on our shift.

Working in the kitchen was the hardest job of all for the girls. We had to lift heavy pots to take to the dining rooms. Normally we did it alone, never asking anyone to help us. I'm sure that's part of the reason I have back problems today. A few of the girls couldn't lift those heavy pots and had to have someone to help them each time. I didn't have time to waste waiting for someone to help me. As far as I can recall, I never dropped one of those large pots of food.

I enjoyed working in the kitchen. If I wasn't there I was in the teacher's dining room as a head girl. It was next to the kitchen and I could walk in there and get something to eat. I think I ate with the kitchen girls at meal time. I do know we didn't really sit down to eat. We had a cubby hole we would sit on stools to rest and that is where we ate our meal. Being a head girl in the teachers' dining room was also something I really enjoyed.

The tedious work in the kitchen was hard on us but all the girls I worked with were so much fun. We always had a ball with Mrs. Harris and we laughed a lot while working. Some of the time we would start singing and she would sing along with us. She was one of a kind and we all loved her.

I know there were some girls who didn't care to work in the kitchen, but it was fun because I learned to cook different things and even today there isn't anything I don't like. I have already told you about Steven Dean having to eat cabbage from his pocket. Well, I got to the place I didn't care for cabbage either. I think it was because I always thought about Steven.

Today cabbage, turnip greens, and collards are some of my favorite vegetables. I much rather have veggies than meat any day. They are my favorite of all foods. There is nothing like fresh vegetables with sliced tomatoes and cucumbers to add in for a great meal. Fry up some corn bread and you have a great meal that will outdo any meat you cook.

Our bakery was in the basement of the kitchen and dining rooms. When I was working in the kitchen, Charlie Gibbs worked in the bakery. I used to love a good piece of bread that

Charlie had just pulled from the oven. It was not only warm, but it was so soft it would almost melt in your mouth.

I loved walking in the kitchen area from outside and the aroma of the bread baking was one that I enjoyed the most. It gave me a warm glow when I walked into the kitchen. I wish I could smell that scent as I walk into a bakery today. I think Charlie baked all the bread we ate at my orphanage home. It was heavenly to stand there with Charlie and eat a piece that had just come out of the oven.

We had bread for every meal. I think we bought bread that we used for sandwiches. The bread that orphans made was used for breakfast and dinner. I'm not really sure about this but I do know the bread Charlie baked was great.

We girls baked the cakes. Most of them were sheet cakes because we had to make enough to feed three hundred and some hungry orphan and teachers.

We had three good meals a day and that was it. Snacks in the cottages were not found anywhere unless someone bought them in town. Of course, I would not always eat my piece of fruit the same day but I put in on the windowsill so it would stay cold in the winter months.

Since I have already stated about the bell ringing all the time, I have to tell you who was ringing the bell when I worked in the kitchen. It was Tommy Jones' job and he was always late in the mornings. When I was working the morning shift, the bell was supposed to ring at six o'clock to rise and shine. I was already in the kitchen working by six o'clock. We had to be there at five-thirty to start breakfast for hungry orphans.

Some days Tommy could be as much as ten minutes late. That normally left me to ring that stupid bell. When I rang it, I normally pulled that cord a few times more than necessary.

Mrs. Harris would look at me. "Don't you think it has been rung enough?"

The bell cord was in the hallway of the kitchen and it only took a few steps to get to it. It wasn't any trouble ringing it for Tommy. We were keeping him from getting in trouble. It just made us mad because we rang it to save Tommy's hide. Sometimes he would be late at the dinner hour, also. That was due to him being a football player and couldn't get there in time. I really didn't mind ringing it for him. He was and still is a good friend of mine.

I was a happy teenager. I can't think of anything that preys on my mind as being bad. We were used to working a half day and going to school a half day. It was a normal day and no one griped about it. As I have said so many times, we were always happy or at least most of the time.

We didn't have the drama girls seem to have today. I didn't even know what drama was because we didn't have any. We didn't use drama to get others in trouble because most of us were friends. There were different groups of friends in each cottage, but we all got along.

We heard about boys and girls when they slipped out at night to be together. After we heard it, we forgot. It was one of those things boys and girls did when they were going steady. There was never a reason for any of us to start drama within the cottage we lived in at the time. Drama was never heard of in my orphanage home.

SINCE I HAVE told about the infirmary and me working with Mrs. Tomblin, I have to tell you about getting our tonsils out when they were bad. This normally happened when school was not in session. Most of the time it was during the summer session when no one had to miss school.

Some doctor from the town of Oxford came to the orphanage and it was like hog killing time. Most of the time the girls' dormitory was full of girls. We were put to sleep with ether during those years. We stayed in the infirmary for two or three days depending on how we were doing.

I remember the first morning we had jelly and toast that was still soft. I had blackberry jam that morning and I just about lost it. It wasn't just blackberry jam, it was blackberry jam with seeds in it. Gee, my throat was hurting like crazy. I didn't eat anymore blackberry jam for a long time.

We had ice cream all the time until our throats quit hurting. Now, that was a good way to get what you wanted for a change. Since it was a good change, we didn't have to go to work for a few days. I simply enjoyed my time in bed and talking to the other girls and eating lots of ice cream. The boys and girls were young when our tonsils were removed. They would do one set of orphans and then another set. I think the doctors were only at our infirmary twice to remove tonsils during the summer months.

Since I am telling about the infirmary I have to tell you about our dentist, Mr. Jones. We had checkups every six months the way my family does today. Mr. Jones, the dentist, had his office at the infirmary, on the first floor near the children's playroom. He had one dentist chair to use. Oh my, how we all hated going to see Mr. Jones. It was nothing for him to grind on your tongue or gum . . . anywhere . . . the hurt was awful. I have heard since leaving my orphanage home how most of the orphans hated this dentist. He came once a week, normally on Thursdays.

Those who had bad teeth got braces. They went to Oxford or to Raleigh for the dental work. My teeth were more or less straight and I never had braces. Your teeth had to be really bad to get braces to straighten them out.

One of my best friends at our orphanage, Arthur Stone, was an orthodontist in Raleigh when Donald and I were living there. My youngest daughter, Rhonda, went to Art for her braces. He started going to the orphanage to see which orphans needed braces. For years he put braces on kids and never charged the orphanage a dime. He was one in a million. I still see him when he comes for homecoming each year. I love this man and he is certainly one of my favorite orphan brothers.

Twenty-one

BEFORE I FORGET, let me tell you about another meal we had every week. On Saturday night for dinner we always had hot dogs, chili, slaw, and baked beans. This was one meal the boys especially liked. I know for sure Dickie Powell loved the Saturday night dinners. We have discussed this several times when our families are together. We hold hands and say the blessing together when we are with his family at the beach each year. It is our orphanage blessing and we never forget it.

I HAVE TOLD about the jobs the girls had while in my orphanage home. I will now try to tell you about the boys and what they did. They had some heavy jobs as I remember. Not all the boys worked on the farm or dairy.

We had our own dairy and the boys milked the cows. I think we had one that was electric and the rest were milked by hand. The boys milked the cows each morning and brought the containers of milk to the kitchen. The containers went into the walk-in refrigerator to get cold before serving it.

Those cows were fed and milked every day. As I recall, most of the boys enjoyed working at the dairy. I do know how good that milk was when it was extremely cold, especially in the summer. My friend Dickie Powell worked on the dairy most of the time. Mr. Legion was in charge of the dairy until his death and then Bob Davis took over the dairy and the boys who worked there.

We kitchen girls would get hot during the day while cooking and we would go into the refrigerator for a few minutes to cool off. We had no air conditioners in my orphanage home while I was there. There was a walk-in freezer next to the walk-in refrigerator. The meats Mr. Pruitt ordered were kept there. We didn't have frozen vegetables then. We used canned vegetables unless it was the fresh vegetables the girls in the vegetable house shelled.

Orphans went barefoot everywhere on campus. I remember mopping the kitchen floor, after we finished cleaning up at night, and taking the mop outside to clean under the spigot barefoot. I did this winter and summer alike. Even in the snow I walked outside barefoot to get the job done. It didn't bother any of us to go barefoot during the winter months. The bottom of our feet were tough. We were used to it and we enjoyed not wearing shoes. I still go barefoot now that I am seventy-nine years old. One trait we learned as a tiny tot and we never stopped doing it.

Mr. Thomas Adams was in charge of the farm and the boys who worked there. The boys working on the farm were also in charge of the chicken coops. Those chickens also had to be fed every day. Those chicken coops were long and chickens shared them together I think. It has been so long now that I don't remember if they were separated or not. Their clucking could be heard when I was outside the kitchen for some reason.

The boys gathered the eggs and brought them to the kitchen for us girls to cook in the mornings and for making cakes and other sweet goodies. We normally had a good batch of eggs each day. Of course, there were not enough for breakfast each day so Mr. Pruitt bought them from a distributor. We had eggs every morning, never pancakes of any kind.

We also had hogs at my orphanage home. Hogs were fed well until it was time for them to be killed during the cold winter months. The boys would slit those hogs wide open and string them on some wire contraption outside the kitchen where we kitchen girls saw them each time we emptied the trash.

They were bloody and horrible looking. They stayed that way for at least a day for the blood to get out, then the hard work happened. The boys would cut those hogs into roast, pork chops, etc. and bring them in the kitchen for us girls to cook the skin.

The grease from the skins was used for seasoning. The skins, after they were cooked enough to remove all the grease, were delicious. They were so crunchy and I loved those things. They seemed to call me to them and I obeyed, causing me to eat a bunch of them until I had a stomach ache.

Then the fat was fried to get the crackling dried out. Sometimes Mr. Pruitt would put the crackling in the eggs for breakfast. Everyone ate the eggs cooked that way whether they liked it or not. It was a change and we definitely needed a change once in a while. Since I was in the kitchen, I didn't have to eat the eggs cooked this way. In fact I've never eaten eggs with crackling cooked with them. All I can say is yuck to that.

We even made sausage from those hogs. The girls would work the grinder and we knew how much season to use to get the perfect taste for serving. We made some round sausage for the freezer and we also made link sausage. I liked the link sausage the best and when we had it for breakfast it was a big hit with everyone. They hung in the refrigerator until we used them for breakfast.

As you can tell, we used what we either grew or raised each year. I think we all learned to like everything that was cooked in my orphanage home. For sure, we never went hungry. If anyone happened to be hungry, I never knew about it. It might be someone who didn't care for some of the meals, but they didn't go hungry, they ate it, regardless. That's why my orphanage home was good for us orphans. We always had balanced meals and there was fruit to eat, likewise.

The farm boys grew our own beans and peas for us to shell and eat. I don't remember if we shucked the corn, but I think the boys on the farm shucked the corn and the shucks and corn cobs were given to the hogs. I just remember all meals were great.

Twenty-two

ON CAMPUS WAS the shoe shop that I've already mentioned in the first part of my story. In the same area was the printing shop and the electrical shop. My orphan brothers worked in one of these shops if they were not working on the farm. Working in these shops got the boys ready for a trade when they graduated from high school. I remember Tommy Jones worked in the shoe shop when we were teenagers.

Most of the boys went to college, but those who didn't had a good trade to work outside the home once they graduated. I remember so many of them who left after graduation and went on to work either in the printing industry or the electrical industry.

All my brothers and sisters had something they could fall back on when they left our orphanage home. The girls had the infirmary they could work at or a kitchen in the city they were living. If they worked in the kitchen, they were used to doing heavy jobs and never thought about it being hard. Not only that, but they could become a waiter anywhere they lived. They were used to serving people because they grew up doing it.

Then there were some girls who learned to sew and they could work almost anywhere where clothing was bought. When we were seniors we shopped for our Sunday clothes in Oxford. They were giving us the opportunity to be ready for a profession. Some of the girls worked in the area where we tried on clothes. It was like a place where we buy used clothing now.

Of course we had the laundry where the clothes were washed and ironed. The girls learned how to iron out all the wrinkles so they would be good for a laundry. I have to admit since I started writing my story about my orphanage home, I appreciate how we were trained to be self-orientated, to care for ourselves when we graduated. In all, we were all trained well and when we went into the working world, we could earn a living.

I almost forgot to tell you about our school. When we became older, in the eleventh or twelfth grades, we were able to take typing and shorthand. I loved both and I was efficient at shorthand. I still remember some of the shorthand. We had a great teacher who taught us well.

Even some of the boys took typing and this would help them in the printing shop. We printed everything for the orphanage and the boys also printed things for the town of Oxford. Each year our annuals were printed by our orphan brothers. As you can see, we could go out into the working world and do great things.

Some of my favorite teachers were Mrs. Legion who taught English and Language in high school. She also taught us the Bible. I learned so much about the Bible from her. She was the most wonderful teacher I've ever had. Her voice was low and she never yelled. Every orphan has nothing but good things to say about Mrs. Legion and she was one in a million.

The boys felt the same about Mr. Legion. He was good to them and taught them a lot about the dairy. He was well respected. They both lived in one of the houses on campus. Of course, Mr. Legion died while I was still in the orphanage. It was a sad time for the boys who worked with him at the dairy.

My very favorite of all was Roy Marsh who taught the eighth grade. He was married and lived in one of the houses on campus. When he taught us History I fell in love with the state of Maine. I did this state as a project when I was in his class. I finally got to go to Maine to see that beautiful state.

My math teacher was a great man. Garland Talton was one of those people you never forget. If it hadn't been for him and Jack Barger I would have never passed Algebra II. Not only was he a good teacher but a terrific coach for the football and baseball teams.

My very favorite teacher in high school was Gabe Austell. He taught Biology and Chemistry to the high school orphans.

He was also the coach of the boys' football team. He was a great person and so was his wife, Libby. They had five boys and we used to tease them about having their own basketball team.

He became the Superintendent of the orphanage when I lived in Angier. He would come to the Masonic meeting and stop by to see us. He was indeed the best thing for the boys even though he was strict. I loved this couple and used to watch their boys when Libby had to go somewhere.

WHEN IT CAME time to graduate, we had our own graduation service on the front lawn under those beautiful, old, oak trees. The juniors always had the job of making the daisy chain for the seniors to walk between. They would stand across from one another while the seniors walked between them. It was a tradition for many years at my orphanage home. We girls had new dresses and I guess the boys had new suits. We were happy campers when it came our time to leave the warmth of our orphanage bed.

After we had the afternoon session we went to Webb High School in Oxford to walk across the stage to receive our diplomas. We were so excited to be leaving that night with our family of genes. When Jo and I walked across the stage our family was there to see us. Papa and his wife, our married aunt and uncle, and our unmarried aunt came to see us graduate.

Somehow our dad heard that we were graduating and he came also. I never thought about how they left us for ten years without any correspondence.

We were already at Webb High School, downtown Oxford, when our daddy walked in drunk as a skunk. Papa got him out the door and told him not to come back in if all he could do was get drunk.

The only thing he ever gave us was a baby doll when we were little. Our so-called loving family didn't offer us much of anything. We worked for what we got during the summer vacation. It was a big rejection during our graduation. Nothing . . . I mean . . . nothing . . . not one thing . . . or money . . .

We left our orphanage home that night and went to Papa's house in Willow Spring, North Carolina. We thought we would be able to stay there but the house was full of Papa's new wife, her girls, and her granddaughter.

These so-called women shouldn't be living with their mother. They should have been out working for their upkeep instead of fudging off Papa. They didn't want a job, why would they? Papa kept them up and of course, his money gave them the opportunity . . . for . . .

Consequently, guess what, there was no place for Jo and me to stay. Papa told our married aunt that since we were home, we could work in tobacco and do other things for him. He had already planned to use us as his hired help and we would have to find our own housing.

The next day we went to live with our aunt and uncle. My first cousin had married so we had her room to share. Of course Jo and I didn't mind sharing a room. In fact it was nice for a change. Our aunt's oldest son was married and attending Wake Forest University to be a minister. They lived in Raleigh so there were only two sons left at their home.

We got settled in our new environment and somehow I managed to get a job at the telephone company in Fuquay-Varina, North Carolina. I rode with a distant cousin to work each day. He worked in Fuquay-Varina and so it worked for me. I paid him for the ride because he had to go out of his way to pick me up and take me home each day. I had a ball working this job. For once I was making money every day. I was in hog's heaven making my own money.

Back then, the person would call the operator and ask for the number. It was our responsibility to ring the line they wanted. There were times when I would ring it back in the caller's ear and then we girls would laugh about it. I really enjoyed working there, but I wanted to be in Raleigh where I could find a better job.

Jo didn't find a job that summer, so she stayed home and worked in tobacco again. She was also battling an ear infection and ran a fever for days. My little sister was very sick at that time and I felt for her. Our aunt took her to the doctor and he gave her something to help with the infection.

A lady in our church became a good friend of mine and helped me find a boarding house in Raleigh to live. She also found a job for me since she knew the woman in charge of the office at Standard Supply Company. It was close enough for me to walk to work and I walked home during my lunch hour and ate with Mrs. Sandlin, the woman who owned the boarding house.

Jo had to take the bus to work each day. Since Jo and I didn't have a car, we either had to walk or take the bus to wherever we wanted to go. She had a job with State Capital Insurance Company.

Living in the boarding house was almost like living in the orphanage. There were about six or seven bedroom, two on the first floor and four or five on the upper floor. In the basement several boys lived. Most of the bedrooms held at least two girls or maybe four, depending on who was doing the sharing and how many beds were in each room.

I loved living in the boarding house. Jo and I shared a bed while Ernestine Harrison, our orphan sister, had the other one. There were only three of us in our room. Of course the bathroom was off our room. I'm sure some of the other girls had to use our bathroom.

We could eat with Mrs. Sandlin if we wanted and she only charged a small amount for our meal. Living downtown was wonderful and we could walk anywhere. Hudson Belk's Department Store was downtown and that is where most of us went to buy our clothes.

There were two movie houses, the Ambassador and State Theatre, so we would attend a good movie at night during the week and then on Saturday we could go to both of the theatres if we had the money for the movie.

It was nice to walk around downtown because that was where all the state offices were plus the capital of North

Carolina. The governor's mansion was also downtown. We would spend a lot of time on Saturdays walking around the capital. Birds were everywhere and people would buy peanuts to feed them. It was a pleasure to sit and feed the birds and squirrels. We loved living close to the museums and the capital. We visited the museums several times when we were living in the boarding house.

Life was good for Jo and me. I was dating a young man from Fuquay. It was nice to go on dates because we had never done this in the orphanage. I really didn't care that much for the boy but he paid for me to go to the movies, mostly to the drive-ins. The drive-ins had decent movies but more than anything else, it was a place to make out, which he wanted to do all the time. I had not grown up making out constantly and didn't care to do it when we were at the drive-in.

He was a year younger, and I met him while working at the telephone company. I don't even know who introduced me to him. I also met some nice men in Willow Springs who I dated. I was learning real fast what boys wanted from girls. I stood by my commitments and would not have sex with any of them. I was saving my body for the man I was to marry one day.

Twenty-three

ONE SUNDAY JO was dating a young man, Jerry Dean, and I planned to ride back to Raleigh with them. Jerry was from Fuquay-Varina and only a short drive to Willow Springs where our married aunt lived.

I needed to get back to Raleigh because I had to go to work the next day and so did Jo. Jerry called Jo and asked if I wanted a date that Sunday night. I said yes because it really didn't matter, I just needed to get home. When he showed up at our aunt's house he introduced me to Donald Lloyd. He was not a big man at all, not much taller than me, but he was so cute.

Well, we thought we were going to have fun. No one could decide whether we should go to the movies or what. We were on Hillsboro Street going to downtown Raleigh and a woman ran a red light at McDowell and Hillsboro Street and hit Jerry's car. Donald and I were in the back seat and that was about where she hit the car. It slung me at Donald and then Donald hit the front seat throwing Jo Ann out. Donald went out too and I was part in and part out of the car. Donald was thrown in the street and Jo Ann was thrown into a used car lot. I don't know about Jerry but if I can recall it correct, he was thrown out the driver's side and landed in the car lot.

Donald and I went to Rex Hospital in the ambulance while the police brought Jo and Jerry. Donald had a broken arm and I was seen by a doctor due to having my appendix removed only a week before. Man, I was so sore from that accident. I don't know how Jerry got home. Probably his dad came to Rex Hospital to get him.

So, now do you see where I'm going with this? Yes, we were now dating. The next night Jo and I went to the hospital to see Donald after we got home from work. When it was time to leave, the boy I had been dating showed up and took Jo and me home.

Even today Donald tells his story about me going to see him and leaving with another boy. I thought nothing of it because we had taken the bus to the hospital and it cost us money. We got home scotch free and didn't have to pay one red cent.

I also met Donald's oldest brother and his wife that night at the hospital. Thomas and Kay Lloyd lived in Raleigh and it wasn't far from where they lived, so they came to see Donald. Kay still reminds me of how it looked with me leaving with another man when I had come to see Donald.

It's a big joke now because Donald and I are a happily married couple sharing fifty-nine years together. Kay was pregnant with her first child at that time. I remember she had on a red maternity top and black pants.

Donald came to see me as soon as he was out of the hospital. Even with that broken arm he was able to drive quite well with that arm across my shoulders. Donald and I dated for over a year. The summer before we got married I went to the mountains with him. His mom and dad invited me to spend my vacation with them. I had never been anywhere except the beach once and it was a nice treat for me. We were gone almost a week and I had a ball. MaMa and I slept together but it didn't bother me since I was used to sleeping with someone.

I fell in love with Donald's family during that year. They took me in as a family member from the first time I went down to Fuquay-Varina on Sunday. Donald would come to my aunt's house and get me so I could go to church with him. It became a habit being with Donald every Sunday for church if I was at my aunt's house. Jo Ann and I would go home to Willow Springs with our first cousin because she worked in Raleigh at Carolina Power and Light.

I met Maynard and Patricia, Donald's brother and his wife at their home in Fuquay-Varina, North Carolina. They had the prettiest little girl with almost white hair. Her name was Kathy and I took to her right away.

Patricia had just had a baby boy and he was the first baby I ever held. His name was Maynard, Junior after his dad. I enjoyed that day so much, being with Donald's family. Maynard and Patricia took me in and I was making my own family. I never felt rejected by any of them. I was a part of this family and I loved every minute I spent with them.

That year went by fast. Sometimes Donald would get out of school and stay in Raleigh until I got off work and I would go home with him. I never spent the night with the Lloyds until Christmas, right before Donald and I were married. He always took me to my aunt's house.

On Sundays when I was at the Lloyds, the boys would get together with friends and play football on the vacant lot next to the Lloyd's house. The game normally lasted all afternoon while the women sat around talking. Thomas and Kay would come from Raleigh and Maynard and Patricia would come from their house and we would have a big lunch after church that MaMa cooked for us.

MaMa was a tiny lady, only four feet ten inches tall and weighed probably wet a good ninety-five pounds. She had the tiniest feet I have ever seen on a woman. She wore a size four shoe. All of MaMa's family were small people but they were big in my eyes. Those Smiths were a great family. They showed their love for one another often.

Twenty-four

DONALD GAVE ME an engagement ring during the Christmas holidays of nineteen-hundred-fifty-six after going together for over a year. We had talked about marriage for at least six months. He was still in school at Hardbarger Business School for accounting. He had finished one year and would finish the second year shortly after we were married. Donald was going year round so he could finish up earlier. He drove from Fuquay-Varina to Raleigh every day to attend class. He graduated in March after we were married.

Our plans were to marry in April the next year. We went to see my first cousin, who was finishing up at Wake Forest Theological Seminary, but didn't have a church of his own yet. We asked him to marry us and of course he said he would.

For a few weeks we went to see him. He and his wife talked to us about marriage and what it was supposed to be like. In the end, my cousin and his wife asked why we were waiting until April to get married. We just thought that would be a good time for us because Donald still had a few months of schooling and wouldn't be working.

We finally decided to get married in February. Donald's birthday is February seventh and we wanted to be married then but Thomas, his brother, would be in New York that week in training with Met Life. Maynard was already working with Met Life. So now two brothers were working for the company. So we set our date to February fourteenth, Valentine's Day.

I only had a month to get things done before the wedding. I brought my wedding dress and it was on sale half-price and it took almost a week's paycheck to pay for it. I didn't eat much during those weeks. I was excited because I was going to marry the one I loved.

My dress had the prettiest lace, buttoning down the back. It was tea length that was popular when I bought it. I also had a veil that matched the dress. I also bought white satin shoes. All my wedding attire was purchased from Mother and Daughter department store in downtown Raleigh.

It is no longer there but I loved that store. Some of the prices were steep, but anyone knowing women's fashion noticed the items were the latest trend in women's clothing. I ended up paying two hundred dollars for the dress and veil. The shoes and prayer book were on sale so I made out like a champ. I bought my negligee there also. Now I was ready for my wedding.

Jo knew some of the guys from North Carolina State University and was having fun dating some of the basketball players. She had come out of her shyness and was having so much fun. She was a petite young lady who had a short hair style. She had become a darling young lady, so pretty and looking more like our dad at that time. Of course he was a very good looking man and dressed to kill. I got my clothing fashion from my dad.

Back then it wasn't odd to be getting married right after high school if you didn't plan to go to college. Well, I happened to find someone within the year after I graduated. We fell in love in such a short time and my life became whole and I was a happy young lady. He listened to me. If I had a problem he tried to help me solve it. He attended my every need and told me about his family and I could see how much he loved them.

I couldn't believe he showed his love to all his family members. I wasn't used to people showing their love to anyone. I loved my orphan brothers and sisters but, at that time, I didn't even know what love was.

I never dreamed I would find the man I would spend the rest of my life within that first year after graduating from high school. He took care of me and taught me how to save money and have a checking account, I didn't have one until we were married. Would you believe I didn't even know how to go about getting a checking account or writing a check?

He knew so much more than I ever dreamed of knowing. Here I was an orphan girl with a decent job and a nice place to live and that was all. I didn't know how to drive a car and had no idea I would ever have one. I was so sheltered and didn't know how to do a lot of things that mattered. I was living in a great big world with no idea of what went on. He stood by me and taught me things about life I had never thought about.

Of course I thought I was in love and listened to him tell me about life and what it would be like after we were married. I had feelings for him but, since I knew nothing of love, I was beginning to feel different when I was around him. His smile, when I opened to the door of the boarding house, was beautiful. He would give me a hug and kiss me right there in the open so anyone coming or going could see him. Donald's eyes were always bright and when he said he was in love with me his eyes shined like stars.

So on February fourteenth at six-thirty in the evening we were married in Boulevard Baptist Church in Raleigh, North Carolina. My wedding plans were very simple because I couldn't afford much. No one offered to give me the wedding. It was up to me to pay every last cent of it. I had my cousin on my daddy's side of the family supply the flowers for me from her floral shop. She didn't charge that much to put flowers and candles in the church. She also fixed my prayer book with an orchid. The church was very pretty that night with the candles giving off a soft glow. Both of my daughters used my prayer book when they were married. I still have it and every once in a while I will look at it and think back to when Donald and I were married in nineteen hundred fifty—seven.

Gloria Thompson sang, since she was a member of the church and her mother and dad had become friends of mine. She was only like thirteen or fourteen at the time, but what a voice that girl had. It was absolutely beautiful. She was Miss Raleigh several years later. Not only did she have a beautiful voice, she was a beautiful lady. I had no one to give me away and no one asked if they could walk me down the aisle.

Papa couldn't have cared less about me getting married. I think he and his wife came to our wedding, but I'm not sure about it. I do remember she gave me a quilt as a wedding gift. It was one she had been using on a bed. It was not a new one and it hurt me when I opened it. It was as though she didn't know me. The same thing happened to Jo Ann when she married Dan Gower. We learned to get over it even though it was hurtful . . . so . . . hurtful at the time. It still hurts today and we will die knowing Papa and Daddy couldn't have cared less.

The pianist started the wedding march and Donald and I walked in together. I was a nervous wreck, not knowing what to expect from my new husband. My cousin had to repeat my part of the wedding vows a couple of time because of my nervousness. We said the traditional wedding vows that a lot of people don't use anymore. I thought I loved Donald even though I didn't really know what love was all about. I cared deeply for him deeply and enjoyed his company and his kisses made me want to melt in his arms. It was after we were married that I learned what love was all about. Today, he is my partner, soul mate, best friend, and lover. I love him more each day that goes by. I am the storm and he is the calm. He has unruffled my feathers so many times and I am still embarrassed when I do this. I blame it on my upbringing, but I guess it is just who I am.

My uncle's sister had a cake cutting for us the night before our wedding. I guess she thought I needed something from the family. She gave me the prettiest cake cutting and Donald's family members were there. It made me feel better seeing MaMa, PaPa, Maynard and Patricia, and Thomas and Kay. I was relaxed because they were there for me that night. Unquestionably, I knew they accepted me.

As soon as the wedding was over we went to Maynard and Patricia's house. It was there that I changed into a suit. I had bought a beautiful navy suit with navy matching shoes and stockings. I also had a winter white pillbox hat to wear that night. I wanted to look perfect for my new husband on our honeymoon night.

I had a beautiful negligee to wear and I knew it wouldn't be long before I would put it on for my husband, Donald Grey Lloyd. By now I was getting more nervous about having sex with the man I had just married. Even though he was my husband I was a very nervous young bride.

Patricia kept my wedding dress and veil until we came home from our honeymoon. We went to a hotel in Raleigh for our first night. We planned to visit Washington, D.C. to see all the sights there, especially the White House and the Capital of the United States. Donald had been several times since he had an aunt who worked and lived in the city of Washington, DC. I had never been anywhere except the beach when I was in the tenth grade and the mountains with Donald and his family. I was so looking forward to see all of Washington.

Twenty-five

IT WAS EXTREMELY cold that night. When we walked into the room it was freezing and Donald had to call the office and tell them the heat wasn't working. We had not unpacked anything, just waited because of the cold room. We wanted to wait and see if they could fix the heat before moving us to another room. They came and fix whatever was wrong and it began to warm up.

A friend of mine, Evelyn Thompson, gave me a pill to take before we had sex to calm me down. She knew I was saving myself for Donald because we had talked about it. She had become my mother in a roundabout way. Her daughter sang at our wedding and I loved this woman. She also gave a tea for me before the wedding and I got some nice wedding gifts. In fact, MaMa, Patricia, and Kay gave me a kitchen shower at Donald's home.

I went to the bathroom while waiting for the man to fix our heating system and took the pill. I couldn't believe I was so nervous. After he had fixed the heating system I returned to the bathroom and changed into my negligee. I stayed in the bathroom longer than expected when Donald called and asked if everything was alright.

My negligee was a beautiful white gown with a light blue ribbon that tied around the waist. I still have it and it fits me even today. Every now and then I will put it on to wear on our anniversary, showing my love to my husband and best friend.

The pill must have kicked in because I became a woman that night. While we were making love I found out what love was all about. God let me feel the love that went from my toes up to my head that night. It was such a beautiful thing and my heart was full of love for the man I had just said *I do* during the wedding ceremony. I would always know the love my soulmate has for me.

We left the next morning and had breakfast at a Howard Johnson's restaurant. Our trip to Washington, D.C. was a wonderful experience for me. We stayed at a Marriott outside the city. From our room we could see airplanes getting ready to land at Reagan National Airport and it was exciting for me. Of course, I had seen airplanes before but one seemed to be coming right at us and it was a scary moment for me.

Donald found some tour guides to show us Washington. Their names were Irvin and Henry. They were brothers and they took us all over the city. We were there for four days, enjoying our honeymoon and living together as husband and wife.

That last day we packed our belongings and headed home. I was so much in love with the man who wanted me for his bride. He brought tears to my eyes each time he told me he loved me. I had never been told by anyone they loved me except my sister. He was going to take care of me for the rest of my life and I had found a family who cared and loved me.

We were going to stay with MaMa and PaPa for a few months and then move to Raleigh after Donald finished his schooling. We were sharing his room that he had been in for years. I was a little uneasy at first because MaMa and PaPa knew what we were doing at night when we went to bed. I was embarrassed at first because I was sleeping with their son. It took almost a month to get used to going to bed with my husband. We were on the other side of the house, but I still felt guilty.

During the month of March I became nauseated and didn't understand why. I asked MaMa about it, and she asked me if I had had my menstrual period. I remember I had one right before our wedding but couldn't remember another one. Hey, I was pregnant with my first child and I was going to be a mom so soon after marrying Donald.

Did I know what to do? Lordy, lordy, of course not. I was learning things at a fast pace now. How could I be pregnant so soon? Well, I couldn't believe God was going to let me be a mom. Donald and I had not talked about children that much and especially not so soon. It was a shock to both of us and in December I would have my first child.

There was so much I had to learn. I had started my life married to a wonderful man and family that I loved. We lived with MaMa and PaPa for four months and then rented the apartment Thomas and Kay had lived in on Wayne Drive, Raleigh, North Carolina. They were buying their first house to live in with three bedrooms. They needed more room with a new addition to their family someday.

Twenty-six

MY FIRST HOME was so important to me. We bought furniture from Cotton Furniture Store, Patricia's family store in Fuquay-Varina. I was five months pregnant and we fixed up our one bedroom apartment with our new furniture and a crib for our baby. Life was taking a completely ninety degree turnaround. Here I was a new bride and a baby on the way. What more could I ask for? I was already starting my own family of genes.

I know God wanted us to be together. His family took me in and I was a member of the Lloyd clan from the very first moment I met them. Now God was letting me have a child to start my own linage. There wasn't anything else I could ask for. I was loved by the man I almost didn't date, only dating him to return to Raleigh. Now we were going to have a child together.

Life was going great; Donald finished his schooling with honors and went to work for Met Life. He worked as an accountant in the office for a year and then became a sales representative. Now the three Lloyd boys were working for the same company, out of the same office, living in the same city of Raleigh. Donald worked for Met Life for thirty-five years till retirement.

Talk about being odd, this was very unusual for a company to hire all brothers for the same office. Donald brought home around fifty dollars a week while working. He would double that as a sales representative plus getting commission on what he sold.

I was still at Standard Supply Company, getting bigger every day. I had gained so much weight, I felt I was about to burst. Dr. Judd hadn't told me about weight gain but I was learning on my own real fast.

The first of December came and I stopped working. My baby was due any day now and I was at home waiting . . . and

. . . waiting . . . I was having some contractions but didn't know much about it. So I called Patricia, my dictionary.

Patricia took me to Fuquay-Varina to see Dr. Judd and I had dilated right much. I was still that orphan girl who had been sheltered for years. I didn't understand what he meant so Patricia told me. I was like a kid wanting to know everything that was happening to me.

Patricia told me lots during the time I was pregnant. If it hadn't been for her, I probably would have lost the baby. She and Kay were my dictionary about babies and having them. They would answer any questions I had on the subject. Now we talk about those memories and it makes us content and happy to be a part of the Lloyd clan.

Dr. Judd broke my water in his office in Fuquay-Varina and then Patricia took me to Mary Elizabeth Hospital on Wake Forest Road in Raleigh. She checked me in at the hospital and after I was in the room, she called Donald. I don't remember much that went on from the moment I talked to Donald.

I remember they gave me something to ease the pain I was enduring. It was a contraption on my wrist with gas to breath. Dr. Judd was a family physician and couldn't do the things gynecologists were able to do with birthing pains. So I had to have ether to get me through my delivery.

I was going in and out, not knowing anything when the time finally came for delivery. I had never been in so much pain. Dr. Judd put an ether mast over my face and before I was asleep I was throwing up. The ether and I didn't see eye to eye on things. I was told to breath deep and let it out several times and finally I was under the smell of ether and didn't remember anything else until I woke to find I had a little bundle of joy, Debra Lynn Lloyd, weighing in at seven pounds and six ounces. Oh, what a beautiful child she was that day and still is today.

After three days in the hospital we were on our way to MaMa and PaPa's house in Fuquay. MaMa was going to look after me while I regained my strength. Donald and I were proud parents of the most beautiful treasure in the world.

She had our genes and she would always be loved by every Lloyd member. Oh, what a treat it was to have my own genes going to this small baby girl. I was in Heaven from that time on. God had been good to me and I knew He would always look after me.

We were now a family of three. It was wonderful to be living away from my orphanage home and being married to the man who would love me forever. I loved my last name of Lloyd and felt I had done a one-hundred-eighty degree turn around.

I felt lucky not to be rejected by any member of this family. I never told any of the Lloyds about the rejections I felt due to Papa and the family. At that moment I only wanted to know the family I married into. What a joy it was for me to wake up each morning and know I would never be rejected, but loved by all the Lloyd family.

I could not have been happier being a mother. I was looking after our little girl while Donald worked. I was washing diapers in the bathtub with a scrubbing board. It was one of the hardest jobs I would do for years. Lynn used a lot of diapers and I washed up. We didn't have a washer and dryer so I used the floor register in the hall to dry all those diapers. Since Lynn was born in December the register did a wonderful job of drying the diapers because the heat was on. Donald and I went to the laundry-mat to wash our clothes unless we were at MaMa and PaPa's for the weekend.

Lynn was having lots of breathing problems with a red throat and red ears. We thought maybe it was coming from the way the apartment was heated and the dampness from the diapers drying. We finally bought a washer so the apartment wouldn't be so damp when I hung the diapers across the drying rack. The machine wrung the diapers enough so they didn't take any time to dry. I didn't have to be on my knees and scrubbing on that wash board to get those dirty diapers clean.

My little girl was having lots of trouble with ear infections and bronchitis. The cough medicine wasn't working and I was so tired from being up with her several nights in a row. I was sleeping when she slept but I wasn't getting the much needed rest. My pediatrician, Dr. Poole, told me about a prescription for cough medicine I should give her. It was a homemade concoction of whiskey, honey, and paregoric.

We didn't drink and didn't have any whiskey or honey. We had some paregoric due to her teething. The only person I knew who drank was Ervin Moore. I worked with him at Standard Supply Company. I called him and he told me to send Donald over and he would give us some whiskey.

Well, this concoction worked well. It kept her from coughing and she was able to sleep. She should have slept. I tasted of it and it was strong, not to mention it had two things in it that would probably put me to sleep. The three of us finally were able to get a full night's sleep.

CONSEQUENTLY, LIFE WAS on a roll, we were having fun and it was so nice when Donald came home so he could look after her while I cooked dinner. We put her in the crib that was at the foot of our new bed and most nights she would sleep all night. She only woke in the morning around six, wanting her bottle.

I had the entire day to be with my bundle of joy. We took walks around the apartment complex where we lived. She normally would sleep when I was pushing her carriage. She was a great litter trouper and didn't cry much. And mother was in a state of happiness because she was living her life with her own family.

We discussed the idea of getting a two bedrooms apartment because it was hard to sleep with our bundle of joy in the room with us. She woke us up a lot so we started looking for something bigger.

We found a two bedroom apartment on Braden Street that was perfect, not far from where we lived. It was nice and I had a good size kitchen, two nice bedrooms, and a dryer. No one could have been happier than I was. The dryer was like having a million dollars. I loved to wash our clothes and especially

Lynn's diapers and clothes. My life was taking shape and I couldn't have been more content.

Lynn was growing fast, she was smiling one day while holding her she laughed out loud, and I was exuberant when I heard her. She was on a good schedule and I never woke her to be fed, she would wake up and smile once I leaned over to get her from the crib.

I was learning to sew, making some of her clothes during the day while Donald was working. I used MaMa peddle sewing machine, and with Patricia's help I learned to make a lot of things, like a pair of light blue corduroy pants for me.

I did well sewing them up but I had a big flaw in them. The material had a nap that I never thought about. So, one side of the pants were light blue and the other side was dark light blue. I called Patricia and she told me what I had done wrong. That was the first and the last time I would ever make that mistake again. I wore them regardless and thought I was something else because I was learning to sew.

Twenty-seven

DONALD WAS NOW a sales representative with Met Life, starting off making one hundred and some dollars a week. We were living high off the hog. I waited until Thursday or Friday to shop for groceries. Donald would come home and we would bundle Lynn up and head out to the Winn Dixie at Five Points. I learned how to buy what was needed before getting those extra things like drinks and candy. I enjoyed the trips to the grocery store so much and it was nicer with my best friend. Donald had worked at a grocery store during high school and through his two years of college.

I still hadn't learned how to drive so Donald taught me. I drove around the neighborhood at first. I wanted to learn so I could get my license. Then we could get a second car. I passed with flying colors and that second car came to our house. Since PaPa worked for Stroud Pontiac in Fuquay, North Carolina, he found Donald a new car and I took the older Pontiac that we bought from Donald's Aunt Eva.

Time seemed to be passing fast and Lynn was two years old and talking like a champ. We decided it was time to have another child, but decided to wait a few months and then try. We figured we had plenty of time to get pregnant and have more children. After all we were very young.

We went to Virginia Beach for a week and Met Life paid our expenses. Donald had to sell so much insurance to make the trip. We decided it was time to start on the second child and it only took the trip to Virginia Beach to get me pregnant. It was a wonderful trip and we had fun with the men and women who were there. Of course we spent a good portion of time with his brothers and their wives. They had become the three musketeers with wives.

Lynn was almost three and we wanted a boy so bad. Kay and Patricia both had boys by now and Donald and I wanted one, too. Two children, one of each sex would fit us just fine. I was pregnant within a month and our baby was growing big in my belly. I knew it had to be a boy because he was so big.

Dr. Summerlin told me that I had to start watching what I was eating. I only gained sixteen pounds so the bigger I got, it was the baby. He never slowed down in my pouch, kicking up a storm and only getting quiet when I would go to bed. It was as though he knew it was time to be quiet.

It looked like I was going to be late with this child. I was having a lot of trouble sitting or walking. I was swelling into a huge blimp, I was so big. Dr. Summerlin had to induce labor. Out comes this baby boy that weighed in at eight pounds, twelve ounces. Indeed, he was a big one. We already had a name for him and it was Donald Grey Lloyd, Jr. We thought our family was complete with these two children. I couldn't have been happier.

JO ANN HAD been dating a young man by the name of Dan Gower for quite some time and they were planning to get married. I was going to be her matron of honor and she had four other attendants. I don't remember if any of our family were at her wedding in Garner, North Carolina. I think our cousin was a bride's maid along with Marsha Wicker, our friend, and two other friends of Jo's. It was a beautiful wedding at the Baptist church the Gowers were members. Dan and Jo went to the beach for their honeymoon. Donald was an usher at the wedding. I don't think anyone walked Jo Ann down the aisle. I'm almost positive Papa and Corrine were not there. As I have already said, he had no use for the two of us. Rejection . . . all over . . . again.

MET LIFE DECIDED to transfer Donald to Wilson, North Carolina to be the new manager. We up and moved right before Kennedy was shot. Lynn was in a private kindergarten in Wilson. Her teacher's name was Mrs. Beland and she was learning things real fast.

Don was three years old and he was all boy. We moved into an apartment that my gynecologist had just moved from. It was a three bedroom apartment and close to downtown. We had wonderful neighbors and we hit it off from the very first day.

I will never forget sitting on the floor and hemming the dress I wore in my sister's wedding. I planned to wear it to the Newcomers Dance in Wilson in just a few weeks. It was a royal blue silk over a polyester slip. It was a beautiful dress and the color was perfect for my coloring. I had shoes to match and I thought I was hot stuff in that dress.

Our life was good and we settled in the apartment. We joined West Nash Methodist Church and got involved with the choir and Sunday school. Dr. James Bailey was our minister and our families became friends. We lived close-by and could walk to each other's home. I had a lot in common with Helen Bailey and I really hated when they were transferred to Roanoke, Virginia. It was fine at first, but we couldn't let them walk out of our lives. We started going to Roanoke to visit our friends.

While I'm writing about the Baileys I have to tell you another story concerning them and my family. Donald was transferred to Greenville, North Carolina in nineteen-eighty-two and guess who the minister was at Jarvis Memorial Methodist Church? None other than our dear friend, Dr. James Bailey. We were thrilled because we renewed our friendship again. Their children were growing at a fast pace. They had four children at that time, two girls and two boys.

Jim left Jarvis and moved after four years to Wilmington for a while. He was superintendent of the South Eastern part of North Carolina. We left Greenville and went back to Raleigh and joined White Plains Methodist Church in Cary, North Carolina. Behold, Dr. James Bailey was our minister once again. When they retired they moved to Wilmington.

So it looked as if someone was following someone else. It has been a joke we told people about our journey through the different Methodist churches and the Baileys. They were our dear friends that we loved.

AFTER WE MOVED to Greenville I happened to be at the grocery store one day and ran into Joyce Belcher. Joyce used to babysit our children in Wilson when we were going out for dinner or the club to dance the night away. Joyce married Sonny Belcher from no other place than Oxford, North Carolina. Sonny and I had a lot in common since he knew all about my orphanage home. He played football against my orphan brothers and he always said the orphanage had tough boys. Joyce's parents were our next door neighbors in Wilson and we became close friends.

Even though Joyce was ten years younger we became best of friends while we were living in Greenville. I consider this fine lady a sister to me. She has been there through my trials and sadness concerning my family of genes. There is so much love between the two of us and if we don't see each other often, the love never stops growing. She is a true sister to me.

Getting back to our lives in Wilson. We were members of the Newcomers Club where we met some of the finest people in the state of North Carolina. I became president after my first year and I got to know more people of Wilson.

We bought a house in a fairly new neighborhood that had not been completed and it was our first new home since we had been married. We had two homes in Raleigh before moving to Wilson but they were not new homes. I loved my new home and my neighbors were great. So many of them were members of the Newcomers Club.

I got into a bridge group and we played bridge once a month, taking turns having the other seven women at our homes. It was so much fun and I loved the city and hated it when we had to move. These seven girls I played with became my closest friends.

Don wanted a bike bad so he could ride around the neighborhood with his friends. So, that Christmas we got one for him and one for Lynn. After Donald and Starling Bissitte finished putting them together they were feeling pretty darn good and took a ride around the neighborhood on those two bikes. Since Donald was the smaller of the two men, he rode Don's little bike. I laughed until I cried. They were going to have a bad hangover on Christmas morning when the children got up early to see what Santa had brought to them.

Donald got pneumonia that spring and was in the hospital for about a week. During that time I wasn't paying any attention to myself and forgot to take my birth control pills. Well, guess what happened. My gynecologist, Hugh Mattox, lived up the street and his children were friends with our children. They went to school together and played together. They had four children and those kids were like stair steps, one right after the other.

I stopped by their home when I was coming back from the hospital the last night Donald was there. Hugh gave me a prescription to make me start my period. Well, it didn't work. I then called Hugh and told him about my situation. He asked if I wanted to come by his house so he could tell me about the birds and bees. He thought he was so funny telling me that because I was pregnant the third time.

Sure enough I was going to have another baby. I didn't want to be pregnant with a child again. I couldn't believe I didn't want another child. I loved the two I had and thought that was enough for us.

I was beginning to have too much fun and I didn't want to put the fun aside to look after a baby again. When I was supposed to be almost five months into my pregnancy Hugh couldn't hear a heartbeat. It scared me because I didn't want this child I was carrying in my womb. I prayed a lot after that and I told God I would do anything He ask of me if He would let this child live. I was never that selfish again. All I could think of was myself and what I wanted. Boy, I learned a very valuable lesson at the wonderful age of twenty-nine.

Twenty-eight

BILL CRAVEN WAS the other manager with Met Life in Wilson. He and Betty became our closest friends. One night we were going to play bridge with two other couples we knew well. Betty and I set up the tables and got out the food to munch on while playing. My feet were so swollen I thought they were going to burst. Donald, the kids, and I had been to Smithfield that Saturday for some reason and I didn't have time to rest my legs and feet.

I started feeling cramps but didn't think anything of it. Betty was going home to get ready when I really started cramping. I had a friend who lived only a few doors from Betty, who was a nurse in the birthing section of the hospital. Betty dropped me off at her house she could check to see if I was having contractions or upset stomach.

She took me to her bedroom and checked me out. Immediately she picked up the phone and called Betty to come and get me to the hospital because I was about to deliver. Bill and Donald had taken their two girls and our two children to the fair in town.

Betty was there within probably two minutes and rushed me to the hospital while the nurse called Hugh Mattox, my doctor. They put me in a wheelchair and got me situated while Betty gave them the information about me. She was so scared she couldn't give them some of the information they needed.

Betty is the sweetest lady and would never hurt anyone's feelings. I have never had a friend like Betty and probably won't ever have one who is as caring as she is. Betty's sweetness rubs over to others who are in her presence. She is a great lady and I admire her tremendously. Bill passed away a few years ago after he retired and they were living in Asheboro, North Carolina. Betty still lives in Asheboro close to her oldest daughter.

My darling daughter was born in a little over an hour from start to finish. She was ready to make her entrance into this big world and she was planning to do it right now, no intentions of waiting around for me to play bridge. She wanted me to be ready because she was coming, regardless of how I felt.

Weighing in at six pounds, six ounces, she was a small beautiful baby girl and looked so much like her older sister, Lynn. God was good to me again and let me have three adorable children with Donald and our genes. How could any woman be this lucky? I did nothing to deserve this new little girl I held in my arms. She was precious from the time she came into this world and we named her Rhonda Jean.

Now our family was complete. I wanted to have my tubes tied but Hugh wouldn't do it until I had four children. So Donald took it upon himself to do the honor, he decided to have a vasectomy. Now we were a family of five and our genes were being used by all three of our children.

We loved living in Wilson. We had friends and didn't think we would ever leave. But as usual, Donald was called to move back to Raleigh since he was needed there. So, we packed up and left the city I had come to love.

Finding a place to live in Raleigh wasn't hard. Building was going strong and we found a house under construction on Medfield Road in Medfield Estates. There were four bedrooms with three baths. It was the house I had always wanted. Nevertheless, I became bored with life, wanted to expand my wings, and go back to work.

Met Life hired me and I worked for them for five years. I enjoyed working, it was good for me. I had a stomach problem I couldn't get rid of. I spent so much time visiting the doctor and finally the surgeon thought I needed to have a vagotomy, cutting the vagus nerves. The surgeon also made a new opening from the stomach to the small intestines. I thought my life would be better, but to my surprise the surgery didn't help much.

During this time Papa died. He was buried on Lynn's birthday, the tenth of December. I thought everything would be taken care of at this point but I was mistaken. During the next year or so one of the farms was sold and Jo and I received nothing. I took Papa's will to my friend who was our attorney and he said I could contest the will, but it probably wouldn't stand up in court. I thought . . . about it . . thought . . . about . . . it . . .

It preyed on my mind constantly. Finally, the rejection I was feeling got so bad I couldn't work. That is when I decided to take my life because I had felt rejected so many times. I didn't want to live, I was in total shock. Now I knew what rejection was all about and it was tearing me to shreds. My Papa had destroyed his two grandchildren. Now he would only have one to live and that was my sister, Jo Ann Adams Gower. I wanted to die and go to Heaven to be loved by our Holy Father. I knew He would be okay with me taking my life so I went for it.

I took a bottle of sleeping pills hoping it would do the trick, but it didn't. I ended up at Holly Hills Hospital. During the time I was there I met some of the nicest people and it wasn't just me, there were many of us trying to get over heartrending situations. There was a lady I met and liked once I got to know her. She played the violin for the North Carolina Symphony. Just about every day she would come to my room or I would go to her room and she played some of the prettiest music I've ever heard. I have no idea if she ever went back to the Symphony or not. She knew classical music was my favorite.

I was there for several weeks. We had tickets to go to Greensboro, North Carolina to see Neil Diamond in concert and those tickets were not cheap. We had paid big time for the four tickets. Lynn and her husband, Gregg were planning to go with us. My doctor finally agreed to let me leave for the night and come back the next day. I had wanted to see my favorite singer for so long. I had seen him once in concert and wanted to see him just one more time. I ended up seeing Neil Diamond in concert three different times. Man, I do love his music.

We had a great time and our seats were so high you could have gotten a noise bleed. As it turned out, John and Barbara Belk were there also. We sat together and then we went to their home for coffee before returning to Raleigh. You never know when you will run into someone you know. It was so nice to be with John, my orphan brother and his wife, Barbara. We are still good friends today and we always get together at homecoming each year.

I was able to leave Holly Hills Hospital after being there six weeks. I went back to work and enjoyed my career with Met Life. The stomach was still giving me a lot of trouble. I let the stomach go and kept taking aspirins for it. I loved my work and got to know a lot of people in the city of Raleigh.

I found out that Papa's house was going up for sale. I talked to my married aunt and she let us buy it to renovate. It was a one-hundred-year-old house with a wraparound porch that I loved. She was going to build my unmarried aunt and uncle a small house of their own behind the big house.

We bought it for almost nothing and got to work having it fixed up. It ended up with three bedrooms and two full baths upstairs. Downstairs was the sitting room, living room, den, kitchen, and a large master bedroom with a full bath. I was having a good time renovating the house, hoping to get to know my family better by living in Angier where they lived.

The back porch was enclosed and it was my laundry and sewing room with windows all around to let the light pour in when I was sewing. I had shelves built in and that was my special room. Of course I enjoyed seeing cars go by, too. It was so much fun and we moved in our new home in Angier, North Carolina in December, 1979.

I thought buying this house in Angier would let me be closer to the family I had never known. It didn't work out the way I planned. We joined Angier Baptist Church where my family were members and I really enjoyed the church.

There were a few people who thought the minister was having an affair because he was counselling a woman from the church, but I never believed it for one minute. Donald and I liked our minister a lot and knew these people were seeing things that were not there. Ministers get bombarded when they counsel women and people have a good job of putting them down whether there is proof or not. Drama all the time that caused people's life to become shambles.

I told several women off when I overheard them talking about our minister in Sunday school one Sunday. I informed them that church was not the place to be putting out drama they were sending to people. I also told them that they had no proof that he was having an affair and they should keep their mouths shut. They were not teenagers and the drama had to go. I left the church after this and some of the members formed another church with my first cousin the minister.

Twenty-nine

WHILE WE WERE living in Angier, Lynn became engaged to Gregg of Cary, North Carolina. They had been together for five years, four of them in college at Appalachian College in Boone, North Carolina. Lynn wanted a big wedding but wanted to get married in Raleigh. I thought about where would be the best place and we decided on the Presbyterian Church in downtown Raleigh on the corner of Salisbury Street. Gregg grew up as a Catholic and the Presbyterian Church was the nearest thing to Catholic we wanted to go.

Lynn asked the minister from Angier to officiate. He had left Angier Baptist Church and was now at the Baptist Church in Carpenter, North Carolina. We got started six months in advance planning everything. We ended up having the reception at the Amran Building. It belonged to the Shriners of Raleigh. Jack Moore, another orphan brother, helped me get it for nothing. Lynn wanted a band so we found one that was good but not terribly expensive.

The wedding turned out beautiful and it was great with the band playing good music for those who wanted to dance. Donald and I were too tired after the first three dances we were to have with the bride and groom. Donald and I reserved the bridal suite at one of the local hotels in Raleigh for their first night together as a married couple.

I had to buy booze for everyone because Gregg's family came from Polish decent and they enjoyed liquor at weddings. I had enough liquor to get the entire city of Raleigh drunk. The wedding ended up being wonderful. Lynn was a beautiful bride and of course I cried when she and her dad walked down the aisle toward Gregg. Since Gregg was living in Charlotte, we helped Gregg's family furnish his apartment. I was going to lose my daughter as soon as she was married. She had already bought her bedroom furniture from Cotton's Furniture Store in Fuquay-Varina. It was one of Patricia's family stores.

By that time I was having a great deal of pain in the stomach. I finally went back to the doctor to find out the acid was eating away at the stomach lining. The doctors decided to remove or tie off part of the stomach that produces acid. So, here I go one more time for surgery. I had already had my gall bladder surgery because the gall bladder was diseased due to the vagotomy I had in 1976.

I woke from surgery to find I only had one-third of my stomach left. They had removed or tied off two-thirds. I thought I was doing great and allowed to return home. I began to have major problems with my stomach. I was swollen so big I couldn't put my clothes on and I was living in my gown and bathrobe. It was hard for me to eat anything. I had lost so much weight and was now down to one-hundred-ten pounds. Finally the hurt was so intense I called the surgeon and he told me to come to his office in Raleigh, pronto.

I arrived at the office and he took me right away. As soon as he saw my stomach he sent me to the hospital. He thought I had had an obstruction of the stomach. They got me in a room and put the tube down into my stomach one more time. As it turned out, there was no obstruction but the food was not passing to the intestines, it was staying in the small stomach pouch. Of course, I wasn't eating much because I was in constantly pain. If I had waited another day I would have had the obstruction. The tube stayed down for days and I hated that tube going from my nose to the stomach. I had rather have surgery again versus that tube being put down.

At first when they first put it down, all this green stuff came out of the stomach. It was rotten food that had turned green and it had become dangerously poisonous to my body. I had had surgery and after a day or so at home I was back in the hospital. I was back for another two to three weeks stay.

During the time I was there I got hooked on Demerol. I could go home once I stopped taking pain medication. I decided I had had enough of the hospital waking me at different times of night so I went to go cold turkey and got myself in shape. I didn't sleep for two nights and shook like crazy.

It was even hard to get up and go to the bathroom because I was shaking so severely. I decided then that I would never get hooked on any type of medication again as long as I lived. I was having hot and cold flashes and the covers were either too much or not enough. When I finally went home, this time it was for good. It was nice to be back in my bed and not woken up during the night for shots or temperature checking.

I wanted to return to work after several weeks but Met Life thought differently. They put me on disability for five years. I had worked for five years and now I would be on disability for another five years. That meant I couldn't work anywhere. I was heartbroken. I loved selling insurance, but I was drawing disability because of my problem with my stomach. When my disability was over I wanted to get back to the work I loved, but Met Life said no because it was too stressful for my condition.

All went well for a year and Donald was driving back and forth from Angier to Raleigh each day. So was Don since he was a senior at Cary High School. We didn't want to take this away from Don since it was his last year. Rhonda was in the eighth grade and doing well at Harnett County Schools. Don graduated from Cary High and was planning to go to North Carolina State University in Raleigh for civil engineering.

We got Don settled and things were great again. Lynn was married, Don was in college, and Rhonda was in the ninth grade at Harnett Central High School. She was getting into trouble and not doing her homework. She had become a social butterfly and having too much fun in Angier. Since we lived in the small town everyone knew what their neighbor and others were doing every day and loved telling their version of the story.

By the time Rhonda was in the tenth grade her grades were not up to par. She was having too much fun and not taking school seriously. Donald and I went before the Harnett County

School Board to see if they would approve if we changed schools for Rhonda to Fuquay High School. Of course they said no because we didn't have a legal reason for wanting to change. Fuquay High School was where Donald graduated from and we already knew some of the parents because they grew up with him. It was in Wake County and Harnett Central was in Harnett County.

Well, that was all we needed to know. The next day Donald called Donald Cotton, principle at Fuquay High School. Rhonda could change schools and she could go to Fuquay High, but we had to change her address. Since MaMa was living with Thomas and Kay in Fuquay-Varina, we changed Rhonda's address to theirs. That way she could live at home and just use MaMa as her guardian if there was a problem.

Rhonda's grades picked up greatly and she was in the honor's group. She tried out for cheerleading and made the team. We went to all the football games that year. The team was winning games like crazy and they ended up in the district finals, which we attended. Rhonda had done a complete turn around and was making excellent grades.

In November of 1982 Donald was told to go to Greenville, North Carolina as a manager. So, we had to pick up and move again. We ended up losing around eighty thousand dollars on the house because it was old and renovated. We were heartbroken because we couldn't recoup our money.

We didn't want Rhonda to change school her senior year so she went to live with her sister, Lynn, until graduation. That worked for a while, but then she lived with Thomas and Kay for a month or so. She then lived with my sister, Jo Ann, for a month before we knew what she was doing.

Rhonda had a boyfriend the entire time she was at Fuquay. He was one year younger than Rhonda, and she was planning to ask Brooks Stephenson to attend the prom with her. We bought her the most beautiful light blue long dress and it was gorgeous on her. When school was out for Christmas she came home to Greenville for those two weeks. She and Brooks had called it quits and she wanted to come home and finish out her last year in Greenville.

After Christmas we got busy and went back to Fuquay High School and got her transcript from the school office. She would finish the last five months at D. H. Conley High School.

While we were living in Greenville Joyce Belcher and I became best friends. We were together constantly during those five years we were there. Sonny and Donald also became friends. We did everything with the Belchers. They are still our best friends.

After living in Greenville for five years we headed back to Raleigh in 1986. We bought a townhouse and lived there until we retired. While living in our townhouse I went to work for Air Products and Chemicals, Inc. I loved the job so much and was glad to be back in the work force. I met some of the nicest people who worked for Air Products. I used to take calls from the home office in Allentown, Pennsylvania and they teased me all the time for my southern accent. I never dreamed I would love working for this chemical company so much.

During this time, Don was dating a young lady who already had four children. He had graduated from North Carolina State University in civil engineering and was working for a firm in Wilmington. He played the field a lot of years and finally he married Dolores Granados at the age of thirty-five. I thought he had lost his mind dating someone with four small children, but he informed me he loved this woman and planned to marry her one day.

So the day came in October and they were married at his home in Wilmington on the front lawn. It was a beautiful wedding and after toasting with champagne we walked across the street to the club where we had his reception. After a year they had a daughter that was named Madalyn Jean Lloyd. She has now entered College of Charleston and getting her college degree. They gave her my middle name and it makes me proud to know she is a big part of me. Today, Don is a single man and having fun dating once again. Maybe there is someone out there who will love my son enough to marry him.

I worked for Air Products for almost eleven years and now I am drawing my pension. I retired at sixty-two and started doing some refinishing of furniture I had picked up for almost nothing. We bought three-fourths of an acre close to the marsh in Southport and built our home in 1999.

Thirty

MOVING TO SOUTHPORT has been great for Donald and me. I love the friends I have made in our church and Bible Study Groups. It's been wonderful and I've made some of the best friends I will ever have.

Donald and I are members of Trinity United Methodist Church and on Wednesday I'm in the kitchen helping Becky Felton prepare a meal for those who come to eat on Wednesday night. It has been such an awarding time for me. With Becky, Linda Lange, and Tom Williams we have the most fun. I think this is what God wants me to do for Him. I am in Heaven when I'm in the church's kitchen.

Becky has been a friend since we met at Southport Baptist Church where we both went for six years. We missed the Methodist Church so we moved our membership and Becky and Bert Felton had already moved theirs. There is no better person than Becky Felton. I love her to the moon and back, she's like a younger sister to me.

Cooking with Linda Lange is an absolutely joy for me. We became good friends and I love her as a sister, too. She became an important part of my life when we met. They joined Trinity United Methodist Church and now Donald and Steve have become good friends, also.

I contribute all my cooking to my wonderful orphanage home where I learned to cook even the simplest of things. I enjoy cooking gourmet foods, putting together a meal is rewarding to me. I would have never guessed I would love cooking as much as I do.

Becky's husband, Bert Felton was a very dear friend of mine and Donald's. We worked with him and Becky for six years in Southport Baptist Church, cooking and serving the members who came to eat on Wonderful Wednesday night.

He had a wooden boat and took people on the river to give them the history of the Cape Fear River. The name of his boat is Solomon T and he is an excellent captain, telling stories about the coast of North Carolina.

Bert was at every Wonderful Wednesday to help us or run to the store for something we needed. He helped clean the pots and pans and sometime he would run the dishwasher. He loved this part of our church, also.

It got to the place I looked forward to seeing Bert walk in the back door to the kitchen and put his apron on. I would walk over to him and give this tall, big man a big hug. Becky has become an adopted sister to me and I love her almost as much as I love my blood sister, Jo Ann.

Becky told me that her grandmother was raised at Oxford Orphanage. This was when the orphanage was in the first stages. I tried to find something that would tell me about her but there is nothing. I really thought I would be able to find pictures of her grandmother but I couldn't. I feel this makes our friendship a lot closer since her grandmother grew up where I did.

Bert died from bone cancer and we had a memorial service for him on Friday, July 11, 2015. Some of my dearest friends worked in the kitchen from seven that morning till five in the afternoon preparing food for Becky and her family and all the almost three hundred and some who came to pay tribute to my dear friend.

Marion Martin is in charge of the kitchen and she does all the ordering of things for us to cook. She has also become a friend of mine. One other lady that I love being with in the kitchen is Donna Albertson. She is always coming up with something unusual to cook and it always turns out to be mouth-watering. Her desserts are the best I have ever eaten. She now makes deserts for the different restaurants in town.

I am going to miss my dear friend, Bert Felton, because he won't be coming to the kitchen anymore. I already miss him and he was the best friend anyone could have. Of course, he will be looking down on Becky, Linda, Tom, and me as we do our thing each Wednesday night starting the first of September and ending the last Wednesday in May.

Bert, when we get to Heaven, Linda and I want to sit down with you and talk about the days when we were together in the kitchen at Trinity United Methodist Church cooking for the members. I can't wait to see that big smile you have and your eyes showing the love you have for Becky when she ask you to run an errand for her.

Linda is the sister I wish I had had while growing up. Linda reread this manuscript so many times and I'm sure she got tired of doing it for me. After all she didn't get paid to edit it. Her life was so much like mine growing up except she wasn't in an orphanage. Maybe that is the reason we hit it off from the very first.

On August 15, 2013 I had open heart surgery. My aortic valve had gone bad and I needed a new one. As it turned out I now have a cow valve that is ticking quite well in my heart. It was scary for me because I didn't even have any signs of being ill or having shortness of breath, it came on as a shock to me. I wasn't scared when they started pushing my gurney toward the operating room. I talked to God and told him I would go home to Him or He could leave me here for a little longer. He decided He needed me to cook for my church a while longer and to tell others of His love.

I woke to see my beautiful family standing at the foot of my bed in the ICU unit. There were my children, Lynn, Don, and Rhonda looking at me. Then my eyes fell on my sister, Jo Ann. At last I saw my beloved husband standing there with a tired face because he was so worried about me. I came through with flying colors and was able to come home and start my life again.

God gave me another chance at living. I am now doing great after surgery. No signs of sickness at all. I feel great when I get up in the mornings. I know I am here for a purpose and maybe I will find that purpose before I die.

Maybe He wanted me to write about my life growing up at Oxford Orphanage. If this is what He wanted me to do I hope He is happy with what I've written. I have poured out my heart to the readers and I've cried a bucket of tears while typing every word of this manuscript.

Rhonda, my youngest daughter, has her master's degree in Administration and is looking for an assistant principle position anywhere she can at the time of this writing. She's now employed by New Hanover School system teaching math at New Hanover High School.

We have decided to sell our house to Rhonda and Jerry since they are in Southport for a few more years. Their daughter, Haydan, is a cheerleader for the middle school and in the seventh grade. She wants to graduate from the school she's at now before going to high school. It only depends on where Rhonda can get a principle position. We have left Southport with a sad heart because we are leaving the dear friends we made.

However, maybe this is what God wants of me. Maybe I can rejoin the Methodist Church in Cary because they also cook on Wednesday nights. I may be able to walk right in and start again cooking for Christian friends.

We have now moved to Cary, North Carolina and are staying with our daughter, Lynn, until we find a place of our own. I know Linda and Steve will come to visit us. I now have several adopted sisters and it causes my eyes to water because the love I found in these women.

Our son, Don, is still in Myrtle Beach, but he is also wanting to go up the ladder. He has a degree in Civil Engineering and works for Dargan Construction Company, building high rises or hotels. So he could be moving anywhere since he isn't married anymore.

Our oldest child, Lynn, lives in Cary, North Carolina and has for many years after Gregg, her husband, went to work with Northern Telecom. They will not be moving out of Cary and we are back in Cary with them. Maybe this is what I am supposed to do. I know Donald wanted to get back to Wake County and I will follow that man anywhere.

Here is the thing about this family of ours. Our children think we need to be close to Lynn since she will never move from Cary. They seem to think Donald and I are too old to be living this far from them.

I have become so unhappy living in Cary and trying to find a place to live. I miss my home in Southport so much and it causes me to cry because of it. We haven't found anywhere we feel like we will be happy living. Everything is so expensive here and it will cost so much more than our home of seventeen years in Southport.

Lynn has noticed how unhappy I am and she called Rhonda to come up so they could talk to us. They now know how unhappy I am and feel we should move back to our home in Southport, North Carolina. I miss my church and my Christian friends there. I miss cooking with Becky, Linda, and Tom on Wednesday nights. I also miss my friends I have made in my Bible Study group that I've been a member of for over at least twelve years.

I miss my home that we built in 1999. It is a part of me and I do want to go home. I believe this is also what God wants me to do. He wants me to start cooking for my church again with my two adopted sisters, Becky and Linda. I have felt empty since coming to Cary, North Carolina like something is missing. I now know that it is my home and returned in April 2016. Going home where we really want to be and yes, I believe this is where my Lord and Savior wants us to be. I'm cooking again come September for Trinity United Methodist Church, Southport, North Carolina. Oh yes, I'm home where my heart is and always will be until that day comes when I will enter the gates of Heaven to be with my Lord family, and friends.

Thirty-one

TODAY I LOVE looking up at those beautiful, old, oak trees at my orphanage home. They now are huge. I love sitting under these trees and talking to some of my brothers or sisters. Some of the trees were destroyed when hurricane Hazel came through, but there are still a lot of them on the campus of my home, Oxford Orphanage.

Hazel, that huge hurricane came through like gang busters, playing havoc on North Carolina. I didn't even know what a hurricane was until Hazel appeared on campus. I was a junior in high school at that time.

We were having P.E. in the room above the dining rooms. Regardless, we were working out and it was raining like crazy. The wind began to blow severely, but we still stayed and finished working out.

When the wind started blowing hard, the room we were in seemed to move slightly. The weather was nasty that day and we didn't want to get sopping wet going to our cottage, the 4-G. Well, it never stopped raining, it rained harder and the wind picked up and was blowing like crazy. In fact, I had never heard the wind blow that hard.

We finished P.E. and walked down the stairs, wondering if we should leave or wait a few minutes. As we walked outside to go to the 4-G cottage, the wind blew so hard it broke one of those big oak trees and it landed on a car parked near Old Gray's office building. We started running to our cottage and almost got blown away several times. We were running against the wind, making it hard to cover much area at a time. We could see those huge oaks swaying in the wind, limbs bending over almost to the ground. The wind made this awful sound and the debris was flying all around us. I will never forget that day and when I'm in other hurricanes I think about Hazel.

Several of those beautiful oak trees were blown over by the time it had finished.

When we got to the cottage we stood at the back door and looked at the huge oak tree that stood only a few feet away from the back door of the cottage. I remember Mrs. Woodruff standing with several of us. Even she was afraid of the tree falling on our cottage.

THERE ARE A few brothers and sisters I want to tell you about since leaving my orphanage home in 1955. These are a few that I love so much and they mean a lot to me. Good things happen when we get together and there are some things that stand out while writing my story about being an orphan. So please bear with me while I write about these few people who have been lifelong brothers and sisters of mine.

First I have to tell about my orphan brother, Jack Barger and what a tease he was to me. Yet, I loved this man like a brother. He helped me with algebra and was also my tutor when it came time for exams.

I could always count on him to make me laugh. He could tell the best jokes I've ever heard. My husband, Donald, and Jack became good friends when we started buying cars from him. He was employed by Cogging Pontiac in Durham, North Carolina which is only a short distant from Raleigh, where we lived.

I can remember when we were in our orphanage home and Jack was on the football team. I would sneak food and drinks to him and the other football players after they were through practice during the winter months. It was easier to sneak food from the infirmary than it was from the kitchen. I did this at both places because Jack and I were such good friends. The boys always wanted something cold to drink before going to the dining room for dinner.

After we graduated from the orphanage Jack moved to Durham and I lived in Raleigh. When Donald and I got married, we would go to homecoming and get together with

Jack on Saturday night, especially at the dances. He was a big drinker and he always had liquor in the trunk of his car. It was there for anyone who wanted a good drink.

Jack and Mary Ann had two children, a boy and girl. They divorced after several years of marriage. Then Jack married Wally and I got to know her. They were a happy couple and their love showed through when we were with them. She was, in my book, what Jack needed during his time with open heart surgeries.

Donald and I enjoyed going to see Wally and Jack for dinner at their home in Durham. He loved to tease Wally, but she would laugh at him, knowing he was playing with her. Of course, Jack was always a big tease. He could tell me something that was the biggest lie I've ever heard and me, like a dummy, would always believe him. If he told me the sky was purple I would have believed him. Then he would give me that certain smile, look at Donald, and I would know he was lying through his teeth. He would start laughing at me as we grabbed each other for a big hug.

This was Jack, the brother I loved so much. His laughter was a joy to my ears. I've never met anyone as special as my orphan brother, Jack Barger. To this day I love that man and hope to be with him again one day.

My oldest daughter, Lynn, graduated from high school and worked at a restaurant as a waitress. She made enough money working the breakfast and lunch shifts to buy a car that would take her back and forth to Boone for college during her four years of college. Of course, we went to see Jack so he could advise her on what type of car she would need.

Jack sold her a Gremlin. Of course, Jack gave her a good discount. That green car, apple green, got her to Appalachian College for two years and it finally lost its get up and go, climbing those mountainous roads of North Carolina traveling back and forth from Boone to Raleigh.

We finally had to get her a new pinto from the Ford dealership in Raleigh for her to finish her last two years of college. Of course, the reason we looked for another dealership was because Jack was no longer with us on earth.

By this time Jack had several open heart surgeries and he was only in his early forties. If I'm correct, he had three different surgeries. He had more scares than anyone I've ever seen due to being opened so many times to repair his wonderful heart. And what a wonderful heart he did have.

He would laugh about these surgeries and when he was wearing shorts he would laugh at the scares on his legs where they had cut him so many times. You could almost play tic-tac-toe on his chest scares. His entire family has suffered from heart problems. It went down the line to his last sister, Patsy, who died in her early years also.

He is gone and I know he's in Heaven looking down on me as I write about him. He was indeed a true brother. I love his laughter and it always made me smile. It was the greatest laugh I've ever heard, not a loud boom but enough to cause me to smile at him.

Jack passed away while we were living in Angier, North Carolina. I was having the orphans down for a pig picking at one of the tobacco warehouses there. It belonged to a cousin of mine and the alumni board thought this would be great to have a get together during the summer months. I was told about Jack by my dear friend, Janice Moore. It was a deep hurt because no one had told me about his passing. I would have been there to celebrate his life.

Jack, I hope you are reading this as I write it. Those earlier days of our lives are good memories of us together as brother and sister. You became a friend to Donald and the two of you would always have so much fun laughing either at homecoming or in our homes. When I get to Heaven we need to laugh together again, my orphan brother. Maybe we can get on the dance floor and do our thing like we did a long time ago. I love you Jack Barger, and don't you ever forget it.

Thirty-two

JANICE MOORE KORNEGAY was my best friend in and out of our orphanage home. We saw one another throughout her life. When I got married I started taking Donald to homecoming each year. Janice graduated from college a year after I was married and became a first grade teacher.

She married Rodney Kornegay from Mount Olive, who was ten years older, but I could see the love he had for her each time we were together. He came to homecoming a few times, but he wanted to be home on his farm, so he stopped coming.

When we got together, either at her home or mine, love was full-bodied for us. We had the love of an orphan sister all the way to the moon and back. Loving another person is so wonderful. That's the way I believe God meant it to be, a special place for orphans to live, grow, and love one another.

That large, old farmhouse is etched in my head and I can see Mrs. Kornegay cooking while Janice and I are sitting in the kitchen with her, talking and laughing. My love for this family is overflowing and I feel so blessed having known every last one of those Moore girls and Hoosie, their brother. What a great family they were.

I can see each room of the farmhouse and especially Janice's bedroom where Betty Jean Moore Johnson, Janice, and I would talk about our lives and what was taking place at that time. We would lay across the bed from one another and talk about our families, especially our children. Their love for me makes me have a warm and toasty feeling as I sit here writing about our times together with tears flowing from my eyes.

Janice never got the new house she dreamed of. They lived in the same house Rodney, her husband, grew up in. Sometime during the eighties they put heating and air conditioning throughout that old farmhouse. They also did some changing of rooms. The kitchen was never very large and if I am correct, it stayed the same throughout Janice's marriage. Rodney died two years after Janice, and Zollie now lives in the house his dad lived in all his life.

Mary Ann is now a grandmother and has a beautiful granddaughter. She lives close by and she and Zollie are still part of my family. Mary Ann and I are friends on Facebook and talk often to one another.

I got to know Janice's mother, who lived in a little white house in Kinston. She was a nurse and I loved going to see her with Janice. We would go while Rodney and Donald stayed on the farm doing their thing. I saw her several times when we started visiting Janice and Rodney. She was a special lady and I thought of her as an aunt. It wasn't too long before she was gone and her little white house ended up in Betty Jean Moore Johnson's possession. Of course, Betty Jean is Janice's younger sister.

After Lynn, our first child, was born, Donald and I would go to see Janice and Rodney for the weekend. That old farmhouse, etched in my mind, was a wonderful place to be on a quiet evening sitting outside the house on the front porch with Janice and I in the swing, swinging lightly as we talked. This would be after we put Lynn and Mary Ann to bed for the night. A slight breeze kept us cool on those warm summer evenings. Living in the country was a great place to be. We couldn't hear the noise of the highway traffic. It was a peaceful place to come to and to be with family.

I gave my dog, Lady, to Janice when I received a notice that I had to keep her tied when she was outside. She was a black Cocker Spaniel and she was, by far, the prettiest dog with black, glossy hair. I didn't want to tie her up so off Lady went to the Kornegay farm where she could run and play with the cows. Janice later told me that she kept killing the chickens and they had to give her to someone who wasn't raising chickens.

When Janice first told me about Lady I laughed so hard, I cried. She was so funny, telling how Lady would chase those chickens until they were too tired to run and then Lady would kill them. Oh how I loved this lady that I grew up with.

Mrs. Kornegay, Rodney's mother, lived with them as long as she lived here on earth. It was her home when Janice and Rodney were married. Janice got along with Mrs. Kornegay. After all, the house belonged to Mrs. Kornegay and she came first. Janice took it in strides, but she wanted her own home, one that was strictly hers.

When our second child, Don, was born, we went to their home in the middle of the winter. I believe Don was around ten months old. The bedroom we slept in was freezing cold. We had to wear socks during the night. We piled the quilts on and by the time we were finally in bed, we couldn't move due to the heaviness of the quilts. We had to put Don in the bed with us because he was crying from being so cold. He was all over me during the night, kicking me or flinging his small arms in my face. Between him and the quilts I was exhausted by morning.

It was like being in a heavy snow storm where you can't move for hours. After that visit we went to see them during the months of April through September. October was the month for homecoming and we would see one another at our orphanage home.

Janice and I never lost track of one another. When Donald and I moved to Greenville, North Carolina, Janice and Betty Jean would come to see us. Betty Jean lived in Kinston, which wasn't far from Greenville. Of course, Mount Olive wasn't far either. We were now close by and could visit more often.

In the summer I would go to Janice's to pick blueberries and she wouldn't let me stop until I had enough to freeze and have plenty to make pancakes, blueberry muffins, and every other thing out of them. She kept me in deer meat also. She was something special that is for sure.

Janice's son, Zollie, would cut wood and brought it to Greenville for us to use in our fireplace. These were such good times for Janice, Betty Jean, and me. Even Donald enjoyed being with them.

We would always get together at homecoming in one of our rooms to talk . . . and . . . talk, causing our voices to become strained. We enjoyed homecoming and it was hard to tell others how we felt about going back home each year. It was an orphan thing and though it wasn't a secret, it was exceptional in every way.

Janice became sick after we moved to Southport, North Carolina to retire. She was in a rehabilitation center in Mount Olive and had to spend her time in the bed.

I loved going to see Janice in the rehab center because I would also see my other friends from the orphanage who also visited her. Our love for each other is so robust, full-bodied and the smiles on our faces would glow in the dark.

We used one of the living rooms to have our heart-to-heart conversations about our lives. You would think we hadn't seen one another for years, yet it had only been a few months in between the times we got together. We were women who learned to love without any harsh words. In fact, I don't think we ever shared a cross word while in or out of our orphanage home.

We went to see Janice several times and she finally died before we could get another visit in. The last time I saw Janice we sang our song we made up when were youngsters in our orphanage home. Even though her voice was weak, she was able to sing the entire song with me. Oh, how I loved hearing her sing our special song. It brings tears to my eyes as I read what I have written about my best friend.

Her smile brings tears to my eyes as I sit here typing. She was such a beautiful lady inside and out. Since I knew she would never leave the rehabilitation center, her love made it more special. There is no greater love than that of an orphan sister.

When Janice died, we were there to be with the family. We were told that we were a part of the Kornegay family and we were expected to sit with them. It was such an honor. Even Patty Jo Cobb Lorah came to the funeral with Jo Anne and Ernestine.

Janice, save some of you stories to tell me when I get to Heaven with you. I hope you are seeing other orphans, like your sister, Betty Jean, Gae Boyette, and of course our brothers, Jack Barger, Leroy Dixon, and Robert Wyatt. Save some of that love for us who are not there yet. We love you to Heaven and back. You are the sister that I have loved since the age of eleven.

BETTY JEAN MOORE Johnson, what a beautiful sounding name. You are my true orphan sister and of course you are the real sister of Janice Moore Kornegay. When Betty Jean graduated from our orphanage home she would come with Janice each year to homecoming. Betty Jean married a young man, William Earl Johnson, from Kinston. He was employed by DuPont of Kinston, North Carolina where he worked until his retirement. Betty Jean worked and retired from Farm Bureau at the age of sixty-two. She and William Earl had one daughter, Annette. When we went to see Janice, Betty Jean was always there waiting for us.

Betty Jean didn't live as long as I expected. She died in her sixties, about two years after William Earl died. Of course we went to William Earl's funeral. She had the cutest home in Kinston. I loved going there for dinner or lunch. It was a place where we could sit in the kitchen and talk. She was not Janice, but she sure was close. The one couple that came to Betty Jean's funeral were Gae and Ernest Boyette. They were my neighbors when we lived in Raleigh. Gae has now gone to Heaven to be with lots of orphan brothers and sisters. Ernest is still living in the same house in Medfield Estates.

Thirty-three

WHAT CAN I say about my dear friend Jo Anne Mitchell Eaton? She lived in Raleigh with her mother after we left our orphanage home. By that time Jo and I had jobs in Raleigh and living there, also. Virginia, Jo Anne's mother had a beauty shop above the bus station in Raleigh.

They lived on Glenwood Avenue in a brick two story building. They had the entire second floor for their home. We used to spend the night with Jo Anne a lot during the first few years we were in Raleigh. Virginia cut our hair and when we spent the night with her, she made sure we had a good meal on the table.

Jo Anne had one brother, Butch Mitchell. I don't remember if he graduated from our home or if he graduated from Raleigh. Regardless, he didn't live long after becoming a man. He was the most likeable person I've ever seen and such a good looking man.

Jo Anne met her husband, Bill Kearney and moved into an apartment near her mother. They used to see Donald and me quite often, especially after Lynn was born. We never lost track of one another and today we still see each other, not as often as we would like but we know how to get in touch, regardless. She is my orphan sister and I love her dearly. She lost her second husband, John Eaton and within two years, her son, Michael Kearney. She is a doting grandmother that is for sure.

ERNESTINE HARRISON GLOVER has been a friend forever. We even lived together after leaving our orphanage home. We have spent many years together and even after she married Bobby Glover.

Ernestine had several brothers who were in our orphanage home as well. She also has a younger sister, Janie, who lives in

Kentucky near her son. This was a fairly large family coming to the orphanage, but there couldn't be any nicer family in my opinion.

After graduating and moving to Raleigh, she roomed with Jo and me. We had such good times together. She went to Troutman Beauty School and became a hair dresser. If I remember correctly, Ernestine and I slept together and Jo Ann slept with another lady who we adopted as a sister, Marsha Wicker Wilson. The four of us were together a lot during that time, living in the boarding house owned by Mrs. Sandlin.

In the basement of the boarding house lived three or four young men. Two of those men became employed by Met Life, the same as Donald and me. Donald was responsible for them changing professions, Bobby Glover and Ray Jordan. Bobby began dating Ernestine and it wasn't long before they were married. They had two sons, Robert and Wade Glover. Ernestine cut my hair for years before we moved to Wilson, North Carolina.

Bobby worked a few years with Met but missed the farm, so he and Ernestine moved to Bailey where they started farming the land. He was such a good friend to us. We always enjoyed being around him and Ernestine.

Bobby started having heart trouble and died when he was in his sixties. He left the farm to Ernestine and her sons. She bought some acreage next to her and now she has quite a large farm. Bobby was my friend and I loved him as a brother.

Ernestine still lives in Bailey and is retired, living like the rest of us. She cooks lunch for Robert and Wade every day she isn't going somewhere. Not sandwiches, but a hot meal for her boys. She has done a wonderful job of raising these two young men. They are polite to others and they run the farm.

Ernestine had back surgery right before homecoming in 2014 and was in the hospital. There have not been many times that Ernestine has not been at homecoming and I missed her so much that year.

We talk by phone frequently and keep each other caught up with our news. There is nothing I won't tell Ernestine because she understands and she doesn't repeat anything. She is closer to me than anyone else in my life except Donald. This lady is an extremely good woman and I admire her so much. She does a lot for her community and church. She is always there for anyone who needs her.

Thirty-four

MY DEAR ORPHAN brother, who tells his children that I was always doing things I shouldn't have been doing in our orphanage home, is Richard Malcom Powell. What a man you turned out to be, my wonderful orphan brother. I didn't see you for years and then in 2005 when my class was having our fiftieth anniversary there you and Barbara were, standing in front of me.

I remember that day so well. Then that night in the conference room at the hotel that I reserved for us to talk, I sat with you and Barbara. I talked the entire night to Barbara and I fell in love with her. She, for sure, is my adopted sister.

We got to know each of you better when you came to our home that spring for the weekend and then later we went to your home to spend time together. We went to the beach together several times and what fun we had. You met Rhonda and Jerry and their two girls when you came to visit us.

When we went to Myrtle Beach you met Don, our son, and then we met the entire Powell clan when you were at Ocean Isle Beach during your summer vacation. We got to know all the Powell clan and I have never seen such nicer people. I love each of your children as my own. I can even name them, Rick and Sheri Powell, Stephanie and Chris Kiser, and Billy Powell."

These children of Dickie and Barbara Powell are special in every way. They have been groomed to be respectful to everyone. They have passed their grooming on to their children and now two great grandsons. I have never met such fine people in my entire life.

I absolutely love this family and consider them my family. We get together when we can and we love one another even with our mistakes. Barbara Powell is one of the finest ladies I've ever met in my entire life. She is so giving and she loves her family in a way that it shows to the moon and back. Her eyes light up when she talks about her great grandson, Mattox, or hears his name. There is no greater, finer, elegant lady than Barbara Powell.

Dickie, Richard, Dick Powell, whatever people call him is one fine man. He is my true orphan brother that I have come to appreciate more each day. He has the most wonderful family I've ever known. His children love him so much and you can see it each time they are together. Dickie, in turn, loves those children. People should see him holding his great grandson, singing to him, getting him to sleep.

If I never had another friend in this life, I would still have Dickie and Barbara Powell as my friends. They are always there if you need them. They would drop everything and come running if I called them for help. Donald and I would do the same for them.

Thirty-five

HOMECOMING IS THE second weekend of October every year at our home in Oxford, North Carolina. It is important to be there because you might see someone you haven't seen in years. It would be terrible not to see a brother or sister who has never attended. Some don't ever make it back, but if they get homesick enough for their brothers and sisters, they may find it in their hearts to take a deep breath, pack those clothes, and attend.

On October 8, 2014, we were packing for homecoming I received a phone call saying my orphan sister, Lennie Everett, had died. Bill Everett was her boyfriend when they were both in our orphanage home. When they graduated from high school Bill went into service and Lennie went through nurses' training and then the day arrived when they were wed.

Their marriage lasted until Lennie started having problems with her stomach. She went to lay down that October afternoon because she was dealing with a lot of pain in her stomach. After five o'clock Bill went to wake her because it was time for dinner. He went to the bedroom to find his beautiful bride had gone to Heaven to be with our Lord.

Donald and I went to the funeral on Friday before going home to see my family of orphans. She had done some great things in her life as a nurse in Rocky Mount, North Carolina. She left Bill, but he is living next to his son which makes it better for him. Lennie was my big sister when we were in our orphanage home. She always worked in the dining rooms as a head girl, at least I think she did. I loved this woman so much and enjoyed being with her.

Lennie, I know you are sitting in heaven with Christ telling Him the things we used to do. Of course He already knows, but I can see your face as you tell the story and then give a big laugh. We love you to the moon and back. I'll never forget you my dear orphan sister and I'll see you some time later when I join you in Heaven.

NOW, ON WITH our homecoming. The Shriners have a parade on Saturday morning. Most people have seen a Shriners' parade and know about the clowns, mountaineer people, and the small cars. They know the Shriners do a lot of good things for children.

There is a barbecue cook-off on the campus starting early Saturday morning. The smell of barbecue sauce travelling through the air makes every orphan hungry. When it's time for lunch we go to each vendor and get some of the finest barbecue you can eat.

There's barbecue chicken for those who don't care for pork. Then there are hot dogs with everything you want on them. These are for people like me who can't have barbecue pork. Of course the hot dogs are not good for the stomach either, but they taste so good going down.

I normally go to the dining room to eat because it is hard to stand, eat, and drink at the same time. Of course, there is a lot of talk going on. Oh boy, most people can hardly eat and talk at the same time, but we manage to do it. It's the most fun in the world to sit in the dining room with our family of orphans and eat like we did when we were tiny tots.

Each year there is a dance on Saturday night but us older orphans don't want to hear loud music anymore, we want to talk. When we were younger we went to the dance and danced like crazy with our husbands and orphan brothers. What a wonderful time we had when we all came together for fun, laughter, and love. No one would sit for long because it was a place of happiness for all who came to dance the night away. The dance floor was always busy with orphans dancing all the latest styles. Those days were fun but today, talking and laughing is much more fun for us older orphans.

Thirty-six

GOING TO HOMECOMING on October 11, 2014, I felt compelled to finish what I had started in my head, telling my story about being an orphan. Donald and I watched the parade in a drizzle of rain and by this time other orphans were arriving. Then we had lunch and did a lot of hugging and kissing other orphans.

Later, around three o'clock, Donald and I registered at the hotel. We went to our room to put the luggage away and headed back down the elevator to see who would show up soon. I didn't want to miss anyone coming through those outside doors while I was in our room.

We would love to see those orphans who never come home for our homecoming because we have a ball. Loving my brothers and sisters is very important because they have given me the love I have in my heart today.

While waiting for Dickie and Barbara Powell, we were sitting in the lounge and I was having a cup of coffee when Bettie and David Braswell came in. Bettie and David Braswell, what can I say about these two wonderful people? David has always been a great orphan brother that has one of the best wives in my book.

Bettie Braswell was like my big sister at our orphanage home. She was first married to my orphan brother, Robert Wyatt. They lived in North Wilkesboro, North Carolina. It's the foothills of the North Carolina Mountains going toward Boone. He passed away, leaving Bettie alone. Along came David Braswell, another orphan brother, who lost his wife to an illness. Bettie and David are now married and extremely happy.

Bettie and I don't get to talk as much, except through e-mail and Facebook. At homecoming, we spent the evening talking about our children, grandchildren, and our homes. What a place to be while orphans vibrate love to one another and then it bounces that love all around the room. And the best part, you never know who is going to walk through that door to join in. That's what happens when a bunch of orphans get together anywhere, any time, and any place. We are like magnets, we draw other orphans to us.

After hugging and kissing these two people that I have loved for many years, through the same door came Loretta Fisher, Bettie's sister, and Loretta's husband Ken. Loretta was one of my best friends when we were in the orphanage together. She was already crying, causing me to shed tears. Our love is never-ending, it goes on forever.

We stood there looking at one another with tears rolling down our cheeks. It was as though we were seeing a mirage. That's what orphans do, for those who don't understand. Loretta has been through some troubling times with her health and didn't come home for a few years. All of a sudden we grabbed each other and started hugging and kissing like we hadn't seen one another in many years.

It was a heartwarming welcome for both of us. Crying and laughing, we finally released one another while others stood there and watched. You know what? Loretta and I didn't care not one iota who was watching us at that special moment in time.

OUR ORPHANAGE HOME has changed so much since I left after graduating from high school. Not as many children living there. Most of the cottages are not being used and sit empty. I have heard it is because there is no fire escape. I guess that's true because there are no stairs on the outside wall for the ones on the second floor to escape.

They have built smaller homes to house the sixty-some children who come and go, depending on family problems. Most of these children have parents who don't want to take care of them. Then there are some hooked on drugs, some who lost their jobs and have no way of earning a living. These children can go back home if things get better for their parents. The state of North Carolina is now involved in helping to fund my home so it is so different from what it used to be.

When I was there, we stayed until we graduated from high school. There were a few who left when one of their siblings graduated from our orphanage home. I've talked to a lot of people who want to know about adopting children from my home. There was no adoption from my orphanage home.

Things change every year and it's sad there aren't more children in my home today.

THE KITCHEN AND dining room are not used for orphans today. We sit in there Saturday at lunch and then again on Sunday, the last day of homecoming. On Sunday we have a great meal of fried chicken with the trimmings. Then we get the small cups of ice cream in different flavors, vanilla, strawberry, and chocolate for desert. We also got these on Sunday before we had the ice cream freezer and Mr. Pruitt made the ice cream.

On Sunday, the last day of homecoming, if the weather permits, we are served outside under the old oak trees. I love standing at one of the tables, under those trees, to eat my chicken and potato salad. Of course, I am always talking to someone. Maybe I will see someone I haven't seen during the weekend.

It's so much fun to go to that special table where the big bowl of peanut butter and molasses is waiting for me. I see the bread and I smile. I fix me a big sandwich with a lot of molasses and peanut butter inside. Y'all, I'm talking about at least an inch thick of that goody stuff between two slices of bread. I wrap it in a bread bag to keep it fresh until I eat it. I always fix one for the road trip home each year. Most of the time it's gone before we ever get near Southport, North Carolina. I do love my molasses and peanut butter swirled together.

Sometimes at home I even add a banana. Now, that is what I call a great sandwich, one of the best sandwiches I have ever eaten. I have to be careful of the peanut butter though. I have a bad stomach and it doesn't take well to peanuts whole or crushed. And remember y'all, molasses gives you lots of iron to make you strong. Maybe that's the reason they gave it to us. It would strengthened our muscles to do the work we did every day.

Thirty-seven

BLACK STRAPPED MOLASSES is the best. I found some in the mountains of North Carolina, but it's all gone now. I wished I had gotten three jars. I haven't been able to find another jar as of yet. I have to take that back. I thought I had found some at the Farmers Market in Raleigh on the fourth of July, 2015 but it was not black strapped molasses.

On August 13, 2015, Donald and I were going to see my orphan brother and his wife, Dickie and Barbara Powell and all the Powell clan. While doing our weekly shopping at Holden's Farmers Market, I notice some of the jellies and jams and an assortment of things made by the Holden family or someone who lives in Shallotte or Ocean Isle.

I happened to actually see Black Strapped Molasses and it comes from the mountains of North Carolina. It says on the label that it's black strapped molasses. Now I know where I can buy more molasses like we had in my orphanage home. Grandma's molasses has always been the closest I've had that tasted like black strap molasses.

In the orphanage the black strapped molasses came in a large barrel. The best molasses I have ever eaten. When I worked in the kitchen some of us girls would go to the basement and turn the handle on the barrel and stick our finger under it and get a big finger full of that good ole molasses. Some would drop on the floor, but we were prepared. In the pocket of our apron was a wet dishcloth to wipe up the evidence. Good eating, folks, if you've never tried it! Try it, y'all love every bite.

The kitchen is large and up-to-date now. It is now rented to a culinary school. Since they don't use the kitchen and dining room for the current residents who are in our orphanage home, it only makes sense to rent it out.

A FEW YEARS ago someone thought about roasting different people who were either in our orphanage home or who worked there. There is now a roast on Saturday night in the dining room with a great meal for those attending the roast. The years have passed and we older orphans don't know the people they are roasting so we don't go.

We ended up at the steak restaurant close to our orphanage home to enjoy a good meal with lots of love and talk at homecoming. Of course, there is always laughter when we are together. There are times when I want to be a fly on the wall so I can hear all the conversations taking place at the different tables. What a wonderful way to spend the last night of homecoming. So much love bouncing around the room and no one is shy when it comes to our family of orphans.

We gather in the lobby in the hotel after dinner to talk and spend time with one another. There are normally around thirty of us and we sit around discussing our lives and our homes, the world situation, and then discussing our grandchildren. So much fun and enough love that reaches up to the moon and back down again. How can anyone not enjoy a night like we have every year?

Of course, some of us bring a bottle of wine and we share it while talking. John Stone always brings at least two bottles of red wine and so do I. Dickie and Barbara Powell brings the white wine and Barbara always brings the plastic wine glasses for us to use.

John and Barbara Belk tell about Wood, their grandson, who plays baseball for University of North Carolina at Chapel Hill, N.C. He is going to school on a baseball scholarship. If I've ever seen proud grandparents, they are true grandparents in my eyes. They love their grandchildren as much as they did their daughters when they were growing up.

The last evening in 2014 was spent with my orphan sisters Patty Jo Cobb Lorah, Hazel Strum Davidson, Jo Anne Mitchell Eaton, Loretta Evans Fisher, Barbara Powell, Loretta Garner, and Bettie Evans Wyatt Braswell.

There were a lot of orphan men there, also. They were Bob Garner, David Braswell, Dickie Powell, John Belk, Dan Braswell, and John Stone.

HAZEL'S GRANDDAUGHTER PITCHES soft-ball for the University of Georgia. She is a very proud grandmother. Hazel told us once the speed of her ball, it was a fast one, that's for sure. I don't recollect the speed, but I would hate to be hit by one of her balls.

Dickie and Barbara Powell have been our close friends for many years. We get so excited we butt in on the conversation, afraid we'll forget what we want to say. That is how much love we have to share.

We try to get together at other times during the year, if we have time to travel. When they come to Ocean Isle beach each year, Donald and I get to spend the day with them.

My heart is always full of love when I see them and I think maybe it's going to burst wide open. There are times when I think my heart can't take anymore love, but guess what, it can and it does. This is my family and where there are family members there is plenty of love to spread around.

Thirty-eight

THE YEAR, OCTOBER 8-10, 2015, I was ready to get to my home for lots of fun and laughter. I get so excited about going home and can't sleep well for a week. I am on a high during the week before we leave for Oxford. People would think I'm so silly but going to my orphanage home is very important for me. I knew it was going to be as good as 2014 was. Then Barbara Powell's brother-in-law died, keeping them away from our special homecoming.

I was waiting for the fun to begin when we went to Ernestine's room. Before I could enter, I saw Bennie Harris Black come through the door. I could not believe it was her. It had been four years since I had seen her. She has been to my home in Southport with Hazel Davidson and Patty Jo Cobb Lorah.

Donald and I went up on Friday this year so we could spend more time with my sisters, Ernestine and Jo Anne. Jo Anne has not been well for several years but when I walked into her room, she had the biggest smile on her face. It was the same smile I have seen for years.

Even though she was sick, her heart was on our meeting again. She has been such a wonderful friend all these years and I hated seeing her not up to par. Ernestine bought a wheelchair for Jo Anne to use while walking. I had no idea Jo was so sick. She was eating very little but everyone was making sure she drank fluids the entire weekend.

It was tiring for Ernestine because she was the caregiver for Jo Anne during the weekend. Of course we all helped but Ernestine knew what to give her and she could tell when Jo was getting tired. Then we went back to the hotel.

We went to the Cobb Center for appetizers and conversation on Friday night. It was very nice to sit with other orphans who came on Friday. The Cobb Center used to be the baby cottage. Billy Ray Cobb decided to have it renovated when the cottage sat empty and now it houses a few offices, archives, and pictures of orphans. It is so nice to walk through some of the rooms where there are things we were used to when we were at our home.

Saturday morning the Shriner Parade began at nine in the town of Oxford and ended up at my orphanage home. It was much larger this year. I enjoyed it very much since it wasn't raining. This was my sixtieth year since leaving my home. When Eddie Dickerson finished announcing events for the entire weekend it was time to sing the Alma Mater. Some of the younger ladies had a ball getting me on stage to help them sing. It was nice to be with them but I didn't want to get on stage to sing our song.

Saturday ended up being a beautiful day. The rain didn't happen, even though I wore my raincoat the entire day. In my group were Ernestine Harrison Glover, Jo Anne Mitchell Eaton, Patty Jo Cobb Lorah, Bennie Harris Black, Loretta Evans Fisher, Hazel Strum Davidson, John Stone, and Donald, my husband.

The afternoon was spent in Ernestine's suite. Odell Smith, John and Barbara Belk came later and the laughter got louder. It was a wonderful day. We went to dinner and we got to sit at one long table and I didn't want the night to end. The room was very noisy due to the conversations going back and forth.

Some members of my class have been taken away and living in heaven with our Father. We figured the girls were going to be the only ones showing up. Then my orphan brother, Archie Capps, showed up at the Cobb Center. He and Ernestine were boy-girl friends at our home. Along with him was his son, grandson, and granddaughter.

His son got to teasing me about the election that is coming up soon. He told his dad that I was not a republican as he thought. Then he was teasing me about loving Obama, which is not true. I had so much fun with Archie's son and grandson. It was really nice to see him again.

Sunday morning, we all went to the chapel to hear one of my favorite orphan brothers give the sermon. Tommy Jones did a fantastic job and we all enjoyed hearing him this year. I didn't know Tommy was a minister. I was in for a shock when he started his sermon.

Was this my orphan brother who was always late ringing the bell each morning for the orphans to rise? He had a good message and it made me proud to be his orphan sister. Afterward we went to the main building to wait for the dinner hour. We had fried chicken, potato salad, slaw, rolls, and ice cream for desert.

When we were finished with the meal, it was getting around two o'clock and we had to start leaving. I really hated leaving but I made reservations for next year for Friday and Saturday night again. One by one people were gathering up their children and getting them in the car to leave. I wanted to stay longer but I had a long ways to drive so it was time for the Lloyds to leave and head back to Southport. As we were going out the main gate, I turned around and threw a kiss at my home, telling it I would be back next year, ready to spend more time with my orphan brothers and sisters.

Thirty-nine

I HAVE FINISHED the story of this orphan, Shelby Jean Adams Lloyd. I was an orphan when I was three years of age and I am an orphan at the age of seventy-nine. I will always be that orphan who felt rejected throughout life by her family, but now I live without letting the rejection do harm to my body.

The orphanage is a mysterious place for those who don't know anything about growing into a young lady without a family. I thought it was going to be hard to write since I don't remember a lot of things that happened when I was a young child.

Talking to some of my fellow brothers and sisters about our orphanage home brings back many good memories. I can still remember a lot of things that happened and where they took place. Even the paragraphs where I tell about a counselor who I didn't care for, I do have a special place in my heart for her.

I hope you enjoyed the book I have written. The love I have for my home, Oxford Orphanage now called The Masonic Home for Children is the best place for children who need the care of others. This story is true according to the memories I have of my home. This orphan is one lucky lady and I appreciate what my orphanage home did for me.

If I had to live my life over again, I wouldn't change one thing about my orphanage home. I have learned so much about myself and what it's like to have a large family. Unless you were reared at Oxford Orphanage you wouldn't understand our love because it's different. By all means, it shows on our faces when we come in contact.

I am a very trusting lady and I guess I always will be. I take people as they are and if they tell me something I believe it. I am a person who loves easily and solid. I will hold onto anyone who gives me a change to hug them.

Since I am such a touchy person, people have a tendency to look at me like I'm crazy. To be completely honest with you, I would even love my enemies if I have any. I cry easily when watching television, movies, and especially reading a book. It doesn't take much to make me cry. My heart is so soft when it comes to people, especially my family of friends and orphans. I would do anything for them.

I hope I have covered enough of my life for you to see how most of us orphans grew up in The Masonic Home for Children from 1945 to 1955. According to some of my friends we were lucky to find a home to grow into adults, never having to look for food and not having a place to live. I now believe Oxford Orphanage is the best place for children to go to when they are left alone in this big world we live in today.

If you see me somewhere, just remember I am that orphan who wrote a book on her life as an orphan. I will be glad to sit and talk to you about my home that I am so proud of. If you have a problem about my memories being factual, just remember that this is strictly from good and bad memories I hold dear concerning my home for a seventy-nine-year-old woman waiting to find someone else tell of my love for my wonderful home, Oxford Orphanage.

The smile on the face of orphans is like looking at yourself in a mirror because we all smile constantly. That's what you call real love for another person. Each one of us has that love and then the smiles are contagious. Smiles are there throughout the entire weekend when we are home for our annual homecoming.

I have pictures on my computer where I can see them any time I feel the need to be back at my orphanage home. I love looking at when I become lonely. Most of the time when I start looking, I go through all of them. While looking at them I'm smiling and thinking how much I love my childhood home.

I get so excited when Donald pulls on that main road going up to the administration building. I want to get out and run around those old, oak trees where all the acorns are laying on the ground. I want to shout out loud and clear so even the angels in Heaven can hear me.

I want to run, laugh, collapse on the ground and tell God how He did an amazing thing when He opened his arms to someone special to start my home for orphans. He is responsible for having orphans come together and being loved by other orphans. He shows His love through every orphan that has ever lived there. He then lets that love show when we get together. God knows we love one another like brothers and sisters. Of course, we know His love for us shows on our faces when we come together.

"It's my home God and I'm honored to be a part of Oxford Orphanage, now called The Masonic Home for Children. This is where I found love for my brothers and sisters, right here on these grounds. There are no family genes involved, but I do love these folks."

YOU KNOW WHAT, love for other orphans is necessary for this orphan. No one understands where I'm coming from when I talk about the love I have for my orphan brothers and sisters. It is always there whether we are together or not. Just talking on the phone fills our hearts full of that special love.

We are special people and we learned to love without anyone telling or showing us. It's there from the time we entered that beautiful main road to my orphanage home until we die. No one can take the love I have for my orphan brothers and sisters away from me. It was there waiting for me when I entered the orphanage at the age of eight even though I didn't know it at the time.

I learned what love is when my orphan sisters were graduating, leaving our orphanage home, maybe to come back at homecoming or never to show their face again. My heart felt empty when these older sisters where leaving me to finish out my years of schooling at our orphanage home. This is where I learned what the meaning of love is all about. My heart was void when I didn't see these people I was used to seeing every day.

These people are my family. Not a family of genes, but better than any gene could materialize. They are my orphan brothers and sisters. There is not one iota of rejection in these wonderful, Christian people. They would be wonderful brothers and sisters if they were deformed in some way and still . . . no . . . rejections from any of us. We can see the love flowing from each of us. This love is a strong love flowing from one orphan to another one. What a wonderful way to grow up in a place where only orphans can comprehend the love we share all the days of our lives.

Shelby Adams Lloyd retired to Southport, North Carolina in 1999 with her husband, Donald. They has three children and six grandchildren. Their grandchildren are important to her and she will do anything in her power to keep them safe. Loving to read, she started writing at the age of 64. She has self-published one book and has three more manuscripts that she hopes to publish soon. Friends have asked her many times to write about her life growing up in an orphanage. She put other manuscripts aside to spend time working on her life. Shelby is active in her church and helps to cook for the members of Trinity United Methodist Church every week on Wonderful Wednesday. She enjoys cooking especially gourmet recipes she gets from The Food Network and Cook, Inc. You can find her at work most days at the computer where she is working on a new manuscript. If she isn't at the computer or reading a book that one of her writer friends has written, she is crocheting more sweaters.